BEYOND THE CHERRY TREE

The Leadership Wisdom of George Washington

To Nick,

Merit rarely
goes unrewarded!

Jim Hodges

James Parrish Hodges, Ph.D.

ISBN
0-9763920-0-3 (10 digit)
978-0-9763920-0-2 (13 digit)

Library of Congress Control Number: 2007907913

First Edition

Printed in the United States of America
Published by Great Leaders Press
SAN 256-3304
www.leadershipbygeorge.com

Dedication

This book is dedicated in grateful appreciation to all those who—by obeying the highest standards of ethical conduct—have created our great country. Ethics is a system of moral values with a goal that gives purpose and direction to one's life.

The vision of our American forebears was to found a free and independent country with liberty and justice for all. They made the moral choice to put the interests of their fellow man above their own personal desires. Gregg Easterbrook put it well, "An ethics of service is at war with a craving for gain."

The revolutionary generation created the United States. Successive generations have suffered, bled and died to preserve our cherished heritage. Every American today owes a debt of gratitude to the sacrifices of past and present generations.

Without their sacrifices, we would not be enjoying our political freedoms today. Those political freedoms make possible the economic freedoms that have made us the bastion of freedom around the world. This book is written to honor those who chose service to country above even their very lives.

Preface

During my 46 years of working in corporate America, I have witnessed ethical behavior by most of our business leaders. There are some however, that have acted unethically. Their lying, cheating and stealing have cost millions of innocent people their life savings and jobs. Their conduct has also cast a blot on the entire business community.

The Enron debacle hit very close to home, and heavily impacted the lives of my friends and neighbors. It is my hope that this book will offer a warning: that loss of faith in the integrity of our business community hurts the productivity that we need to compete in the global economy. If things continue as they are, we will lose more jobs offshore and go ever deeper into debt.

There is one American man who provides an outstanding ethical role model and mentor. That man is George Washington. By his extraordinary number of contributions to our country, he proves that "nice guys do finish first." Although many books have been written about our first President, this book is unique, for it tells stories of how his ethical behavior shone as a beacon in the creation of our great country. It presents case studies of how modern business leaders have used ethical principles with great success, I offer this book as proof that ethical behavior pays big dividends.

While this book is written in language for the business leader, the principles are valuable for anyone raising a family, teaching school, working in government or in any area of society. This book proves with many true-life examples that ethics in business yields tangible bottom line results.

My hope is that you will find some nuggets of wisdom in these pages. If you can achieve greater business success by helping others lead happier and more fulfilling lives through their work, I will have achieved my goal.

Acknowledgements

I am grateful to the many individuals who have helped in the creation of this book. First among these is my wife, Bonnie Hodges, for her unflagging patience and magnificent illustrations. Our daughter, Cynthia, has given very helpful comments and suggestions throughout this process. My daughter, Jennifer Hodges contributed valuable advice and information.

Others who have made an important contribution to this work are Joyce Everhart; Andy Curtis; Imogene Bryan; Allan Abedor, Ph.D.; Frank Praytor; Ken Nishimura; Art Lambert, Jr., M.D.; Jim Glass; Fred Pearson, CPA; Tom Kraycirik; Russ Abolt; Ann Sloan; Dave Alexander; Ed Cotham, Jr.; and Joe Sommerville, Ph.D. I hope they are proud of the part they have played in bringing George Washington's principles back to life. Special thanks go to Mitchel Whitington, author of many books and editor of many more. His patient guidance through the process from manuscript to the finished product you hold in your hand was more than helpful, it was downright necessary.

A special tribute goes to Barbara Malone, editor "extraordinaire," without whose help and inspiration this book would have languished forever in my head.

James Parrish Hodges, Ph.D.
Houston, Texas
December 2007

Table of Contents

Table of Illustrations

Introduction

Many American adults think that the "Legend of the Cherry Tree" is merely a child's story. While the story has become a hallmark of American folklore and the importance of honesty, it does not end there. George Washington's entire life portrays excellent lessons in the development of ethical and moral leadership.

The United States Senate issued this proclamation a few days after the death of George Washington on Dec 14, 1799. "Let his countrymen forever consecrate the memory of the heroic general, the patriotic citizen and the virtuous statesman. Let them teach their children never to forget that the fruits of his labors and his examples are their inheritance."

To the present day, Washington serves his country, for his life is a substantial reservoir of practical knowledge that leaders today can use to become even more effective. Personal development is the first step to more effective leadership. If one yearns to be the best leader then one should learn from the best. Only leaders can teach leadership.

The ethical behavior of American business is in a woeful state. The goal of this book is to rediscover the ethical principles practiced by George Washington and offer practical application guidelines for the American business community. The intention of the author is to analyze five issues facing American management by means of historical and contemporary anecdotes, in the hope of providing illumination and guidance for more ethical behavior.

Washington was the most productive of American leaders. Here is a list of his major accomplishments:

- Commander-in-chief of the Continental Army, a bunch of rag-tag farm boys that he led to victory over the strongest country in the world, Great Britain;

- President of the Constitutional Convention, which body authored the finest document ever seen for the governance of men—the American Constitution;
- First President of the United States—Washington served for eight years, setting precedents and standards for the most important position in the world.

Washington was the transformational leader who raised the United States from a third-rate colonial supplier of raw material to a free and independent nation that would become the strongest in the world. For these feats he is rightly known as "Father of our Country."

Not so well known, however, is Washington's business acumen. He raised himself up from relative poverty to become one of the wealthiest men in America as CEO of "Enterprise Mt. Vernon." That is where he started learning the leadership principles that served him so well during his public service. We can all profit from his example.

Washington's principles are easily transferable. You, your work force, your family, and your friends can learn and apply them. Your reward will be increased productivity in all your endeavors. Today's senior executives of every enterprise—and those aspiring to that office—can become more effective leaders by taking a page from Washington's book.

As Washington wrote to John Jay in 1788, "I trust we are not too proud or too old to profit by the experience of others." In these pages you will find examples from both the life of George Washington and from contemporary American leaders of the 21st Century.

Albert Schweitzer said, "At times our own light goes out and is replaced by a spark from another person. Each of us has cause to think with deep gratitude of those who have lighted the flame within us."

One could find no finer spark than George Washington.

Washington Signing the Constitution

Chapter One – Leadership At Every Level

The effective leader is a skillful communicator. General Washington wrote one of the finest documents ever produced on leadership. It was in response to a request from Colonel William Woodford at the beginning of the Revolutionary War. Woodford had asked his commander's advice on the proper conduct necessary to be the most effective leader of men. Washington advised him:

"The best general advice I can give is to be strict in your discipline, that is, to require nothing unreasonable of your officers and men, but see that whatever is required be punctually complied with. Reward and punish every man according to his merit, without partiality or prejudice; hear his complaints, if well founded, redress them, if otherwise, discourage them in order to prevent frivolous ones. Discourage vice in every shape, and impress upon the mind of every man from the first to the lowest, of the importance of our cause, and

what it is they are contending for. Forever keep in view the necessity of guarding against surprise. Be plain and precise in your orders, and keep copies of them to refer to, that no mistakes may happen. Be easy and condescending in your deportment to your officers, but not too familiar, lest you subject yourself to a want of that respect, which is necessary to support a proper command. These, Sir, I have presumed to give as the great outlines for your conduct. Signed, Geo Washington."

President Dwight D. Eisenhower said, "Leadership is getting other people to do work because they want to."

Harry Truman described the need for leadership when he wrote, "Men make history, and not the other way around. In periods where there is no leadership, society stands still. Progress occurs when courageous, skillful leaders seize the opportunity to change things for the better."

Effective leadership should exist within the entire company—not just at the top. Everyone should be involved in the leadership process. Old-style leadership of command and control puts a company's future at risk, because it can't adapt fast enough to meet global competition.

The new process of "collective leadership" is fast-acting. Only results count—not the time worked nor the energy expended, as compared with the sales process, in which only the sales count.

More and more big corporations are adopting the collective leadership process. They divide themselves into entrepreneurial units with teams set up to start and finish the process. While called a "new style," it resembles the way things worked before assembly line production. This new style of leadership is a transformation change that many accept readily.

Effective leadership within this new process listens to advice from workers, takes and gives critique, but does not criticize, is not cynical, creates enthusiasm and not fear, and trusts the workers to behave ethically. Leaders create the corporate culture in which work is done—the better the environment, the greater the productivity.

The new style collective leader seeks 360-degree feedback—that is, comments from every stakeholder around the spectrum. Under the old style of command and control leadership, workers didn't dare show weakness. It would be held against them, even grounds for dismissal. Under the new style leadership, they are even encouraged to do so. Admitting they need help will best assure that the work will be done—correctly.

Will it be easy for you to become a more effective leader? No! Will your effort be worth it? Yes!

As George Washington's contemporary, Thomas Paine—the author first of *Common Sense* and later, *American Crisis*—wrote, "The harder the conflict, the more glorious the triumph. What we obtain too cheap, we esteem too lightly; it is dearness only that gives everything its value. I love the man that can smile in trouble, that can gather strength from distress and grow brave by reflection. 'Tis the business of little minds to shrink; but he whose heart is firm, and whose conscience approves his conduct, will pursue his principles unto death." America is hungry for this type of leadership.

Between a stimulus and a response, there is a moment in which one must make a choice of what action one will take. The more thoroughly ingrained the ethical leadership principles are within us, the more likely we will choose to act correctly.

American companies could earn hundreds of billions of extra dollars each year and improve productivity by implementing Washington's business leadership practices. Washington's accomplishments stemmed from his ability to turn complexity into simplicity. His leadership and management skills had different focuses. He believed that one leads people and manages processes. Leaders do the right things. Managers do things right. The key to his success lay in his ability to distinguish between the two and to give each its due respect.

George Washington speaks:

I am a fourth-generation American. My great-grandfather immigrated to Virginia in the 1650s and started a family of planters. My father died when I was only 11 years old. My mother never remarried so I learned leadership at an early age by helping her to raise my younger sister and three younger brothers. My father had willed his best farm, to his oldest son, my half-brother, Lawrence, who renamed it "Mount Vernon." The next best farm went to Austin, 12 years my senior. I inherited the poorest—Ferry Farm—in Fredericksburg, about 45 miles south of Mount Vernon.

The farm was our sole source of subsistence. We had enough to eat, but we lacked many of the pleasant amenities of life. Contrary to public opinion, I was not born with a silver spoon in my mouth and I couldn't afford to continue school after my father's death. I only received about eight years of formal education. With my mother's encouragement, however, I made up for it by becoming a life-long learner.

Like many poor young men, I developed a fierce ambition to become wealthy. There was no way I could get the formal education necessary to become a lawyer or doctor. I studied surveying, which at that time was equal in money and prestige to those two other honored professions. I became a licensed surveyor for Culpepper Co at age 17—it was my first public office. Here's where I began to learn the business skills so helpful to me in later life. At that young age, I made more money than did the highest paid lawyers in Virginia. I was well on my way to financial independence.

I managed to carve out a niche market for myself. Although I surveyed some lots in the new city of Alexandria, I specialized in surveying large tracts out in the western wilderness of Virginia. Living and working conditions there were difficult. Since I could not do the work alone, I hired and trained a team of assistants. I kept them highly motivated by paying them well and showing my appreciation for their work.

Although I charged high fees, people clamored for my services. They trusted me, for I always told them the truth, was honest in all my measurements, fair in all my dealings—always acting with integrity and honoring my commitments in my service to them. They knew I would be meticulously correct; the last thing a landowner wanted was for the survey of his land to be successfully challenged. I performed 199 surveys and, to my knowledge, not one was ever overturned. I was chiefly paid in cash, but sometimes I received a portion of the tract in kind. That's when I began to accumulate land ownership which was the recognized standard of wealth in colonial Virginia.

I valued what people thought of me. Not only did I want to be a man of substance, I also wanted to be regarded as an ethical and honorable man. When appointed Commander-in-Chief of the Army in June 1775, I wrote my brother-in-law, Burwell Basset, "Reputation derives its principal support from success." I felt confident that—if I applied myself diligently—I could accomplish whatever I attempted.

Other Americans could do the same. I wrote Benjamin Harrison (then Governor of Virginia, the father of one President, and the great grand father of another) on Oct 10, 1784, "A people... who are possessed of the spirit of commerce, who see and who will pursue their advantages, may achieve almost anything."

During my teen years, I spent a lot of time visiting my half-brother, Lawrence, at Mount Vernon. I used some of the money I earned from surveying to join with him in the Ohio Company—a joint venture formed by prominent Virginians. We bought land in the Ohio Valley, with the intention of selling or leasing it.

When Lawrence felt certain in 1751 that he was dying of consumption, he appointed me as his executor and died shortly thereafter. As he had been involved in many business ventures, my duties in settling his estate taught me much about the intricacies of business. I was 19 years old at the time.

Lawrence's will left a life estate to his widow and an outright ownership of Mount Vernon to his children—if any survived her. At the death of them all, Mount Vernon would go to me as residual beneficiary.

Martha Custis, a wealthy widow with two small children, and I were married in January 1759. I helped Martha administer her estate and her children's inheritance. Not only did I pay for the children's needs out of their portion, but I doubled their assets in the first 12 years. We lived at Mount Vernon under lease from Lawrence's estate.

In 1761, when I was 29 years old, Lawrence's widow, Ann, died. I inherited outright ownership of Mount Vernon—2000 acres with a seven-room farmhouse. Owning this estate elevated me to the top tier of Virginia society.

My inheritance was fortuitous for American history, because Mount Vernon lay on the main route north to south in the American colonies. Many distinguished people visited me for extended periods of time. Fortunately, I was wealthy enough to afford that much hospitality. Over time—from participating in countless discourses on political matters—I became skilled at persuading others to my way of thinking.

After inheriting Mount Vernon, my analysis of the farming records showed me that it was losing money by concentrating on raising tobacco, a very labor-intensive crop that rapidly depletes the soil. Losses were also partly due to unfairness in the way the British treated colonials. Their system was a monopoly, which was rigged against colonial tobacco planters. They restricted the market price for tobacco and in turn charged outrageous prices for finished goods.

They controlled these prices by prohibiting Americans from manufacturing finished goods. The combination of these two factors caused many planters to sink ever deeper into debt until they lost their land to tax foreclosure. I determined never to be among them. These memories made me especially diligent later on as President, ensuring that America had free trade.

I became one of the first plantation owners in Virginia

to switch our fields from tobacco to wheat, corn, flax, hemp and other staples for sale to local consumers. Changing from planter to farmer lowered my social status, but the trade off was well worth it. I turned Mount Vernon from a loss position into a profitable enterprise.

I had to provide food, clothing and shelter for over 400 individuals at Mount Vernon. Pride in work habits and efficiency were my driving forces in satisfying this responsibility. By developing an efficient system of land management, I became America's first large-scale scientific farmer. I learned all I could about every phase of farming—crops, livestock and soils. I subscribed to the leading British agricultural journals and corresponded regularly with their writers and editors.

In my zeal to discover the most productive land use for maximum crop yields, I conducted many experiments in my specially built greenhouses. One study involved ten 100-square-foot plots. This research involved studying the mixture of different soils, water input and various types and amounts of fertilizer. My careful record keeping showed me which combination was most productive.

I was very early among Americans to practice crop rotation, first on a three-year plan and later on the more beneficial seven-year cycle. On a rotating basis I allowed fields to lie fallow. I would plow under crops, particularly clover, to enrich the soil. Visitors and residents alike at Mount Vernon were encouraged, when they saw a pile of manure, to scope it up and toss it into the nearest compost pile. I was one of the first farmers to foster the use of lime as a chemical fertilizer.

I was challenging the "status quo" when I conducted all those agricultural experiments. I was proactive in trying to bring about positive improvements in the environment at my beloved Mount Vernon.

I was very fond of pineapples and ate them with many meals. I built a unique green house for raising them as well as other exotic tropical plants. It had windows from ceiling to floor to let in sunlight. They were shuttered every evening, however, to keep in the heat. I had fireplaces connected to under floor passageways for the hot air to flow under the plants to keep them warm. My methods proved very successful.

Mount Vernon was more than just a farm. We engaged in many business enterprises as well. I opened a gristmill for our own use, but soon enlarged it for public use. I installed first a coarse and then later a fine grindstone to sell the flour to a broader market. We had a sawmill, cloth factory, dairy, smokehouse, vineyard and cider press on the property as well.

I invented a special type of plow that was more efficient, for it did double duty—dropping seeds as it plowed. If America had had a patent office at the time, I probably would have been awarded one.

I built an unusual two-story threshing structure with narrow slats in the floor. As the horses walked over it, the smaller wheat kernels would fell through to the bottom floor while the larger chaff remained behind for easy removal.

I bought a schooner and successfully fished commercially in the Potomac, netting in one year nearly a million fish. Many of these were kept for home consumption, but I had the rest salted, put into barrels—which I had made in my own cooperage business—and sold down in the West Indies. We also developed a successful stock breeding operation and some have called me the "father of the American mule."

Later, after I had returned from the presidency, I built a distillery producing 12,000 gallons of whiskey annually making me America' s largest distiller at the time.

All the while, I successfully speculated in land. All these business ventures helped prepare me for my later duties as a public servant. Beginning at age 17 and continuing on until age 43—when I became Commander-in-Chief of the Continental Army, my business success transformed me from enjoying a relatively modest standard of living into becoming one of wealthiest men in America.

What I did not know or could not learn myself, I sought help from others and put their knowledge to good use. I was one of the first Americans to conduct time and motion studies. At Mount Vernon, a four-man team of my workmen were averaging about 120 board feet of sawed lumber a day. I thought this production was much too low. I decided to spend a day watching and working with them. It soon became evident that they were grossly inefficient. I started instructing them on methods to improve production. That day they cut 400 board feet. As I could not keep supervising them their production gradually dwindled back to the original 120 board feet. Referring back upon that incident, I advised my adopted son, "Wash" Custis, in a letter dated 7 January 1798, "System in all things should be aimed at, for in execution it renders everything more easy."

When I inherited Mount Vernon, it was a relatively modest estate. Over the next forty years, however, I lavished time, money and attention on enlarging and refurbishing it. Ultimately the mansion became what you see today. The acreage grew to over 8000. I divided it up into five farms each with its own manager. Most often, the managers were slaves to whom I gave great responsibility. I trusted them and rewarded them appropriately for their duties. These five would in turn regularly report to a single overseer. Then on Saturdays the overseer and I would review progress on the farms.

I would lay out plans—often a year in advance—for the necessary tasks. I prioritized the work in order of importance, emphasizing careful attention to details. I hated mistakes and wasted time.

On 21 December 1797, I wrote to James Anderson, "The man who does not estimate time as money will forever miscalculate. Much time and much labor are saved by this means. More work will be done in the 'sometimes' when people are steadily at it than when they are taken from and then return to it. If a person only sees and directs from day to day what is to be done, business will not go as well as with a longer term perspective. To deliberate maturely and execute promptly is the way to conduct business to advantage."

In this same vein, I wrote this advice to my nephew, George Steptoe Washington, in December of 1790, "Every hour misspent is lost forever... future years cannot compensate for lost days."

While away from Mount Vernon for over 16 ½ years—first as a general and then as our first President—I continually wrote letters of instruction to my overseers to ensure my estate was managed efficiently. During the war, this attention to Mount Vernon helped focus my mind away from the turmoil. I was also optimistic that someday I would return to live under my 'own vine and fig tree' at Mount Vernon.

George Washington and His Family

W. Edwards Deming wrote of a leader's need to learn. "Learning is not compulsory," he said. "Neither is survival."

American business suffers today for the lack of educated leaders. In the Industrial Revolution, most work required trained people doing repetitive tasks. Today's information technology work force should not only be trained but also educated. Education teaches people to think for themselves. Schools today have, in many cases, mistakenly attempted to educate their students by using training techniques. Students are tested by using true or false and multiple-choice questions, rather than by essay. The old blue book essay test system encouraged students to think to formulate their answers. By delving into and exploring the nuances of the subject matter, they acquired a fuller understanding of the topic.

The word "educatus" is Latin for "to draw out; to question, to bring out the essence of something; to dig deeply into the heart of a matter; to learn all there is about a subject." Since our school system is not doing this adequately, American industry must assume the responsibility for educating our future leaders.

Each year American businesses spend a prodigious amount of money on what is called "leadership training." They should re-focus some of these resources on leadership education.

George Washington speaks:

My broad education and wide reading and reflection upon my own and other's experiences had prepared me to find new opportunities and strategies the better to fulfill my vision. To remain effective, I continued to read and reflect.

I didn't confuse training with education, for they are divergent disciplines. As valuable as training is for managers, education is what develops leaders. Training is learning how to apply what is considered the one best method. For leadership roles, training—because it by rote—is counterproductive and stifles creative thinking.

I had my soldiers trained in drill. Von Steuben was the prime example of a most effective trainer. I personally took the lead in educating my officers—first of all to become good soldiers. Beyond that, I was convinced that we needed to look much farther ahead. There would come a day when we would need civilian leaders of a free and independent nation. I wanted my men to be prepared to fulfill those roles as well.

I encouraged others to become self-learners. I knew that much of the value of the search for knowledge was in the process of learning itself, not simply in the knowledge gained. The process encouraged innovation and creativity, which enabled us not only to survive, but even to grow during our periods of drastic change. Education encourages flexible thinking. Training cannot cope with change because it only offers a fixed answer to the challenges presented.

As President, I tried to get Congress to approve a national university. Young men from all over the country would attend and learn Americanism. My young friend, Congressman James Madison, (later our fourth President), submitted a bill to create such a institution, but it lost by one vote. In this I felt that Congress was short-sighted, but I could do nothing. It is a good example of the power of each vote.

Knowing that leaders owe the highest levels of competency possible to their followers, I did all that I could to prepare myself for my leadership roles. I read widely, analyzed history, and reflected upon my experiences. I eagerly participated in discussion groups that generated diverse opinions. Every aspect of life fascinated me. The dinner table at Mount Vernon was an educational format "par excellence," where my guests and I would linger for hours after dinner, discussing timely topics of interest. At all my military camps—even at Valley Forge—I fostered lively discussion groups, particularly with my younger well-educated officers.

The most effective leaders are also mentors to their followers. Mentors should spend much of their time explaining their vision, mission and values to their followers. Followers must be educated on their role within the vision. Mentor leaders elicit the best from their followers by teaching and inspiring them to operate at their maximum level. Great mentors like Washington expanded their followers' horizons by providing a motivational environment. Great leaders prepare the next generation to be capable of continuing the pursuit of their jointly shared vision. Those mentored owe loyalty to their mentors.

Superiors often stymie junior leaders who are trying to rise in the ranks. These aspirants trying to do their best to serve those that report to them, may go beyond generally accepted behavior. Senior officers, often misunderstanding, may demote, write bad efficiency reports, or even fire these young leaders viewing them as not being 'team players'. But in reality, these junior executives are only doing what all ethical leaders should strive to do. That is, to do the best for those below them for whom they feel responsible.

George Washington speaks:

As a young officer in command of all the Virginia forces in the French and Indian War, I faced the same problem that plagues many mid-level leaders today. My primary duty was to best serve my Virginia troops. This often required my resisting arbitrary British authority. Naturally, my behavior occasionally incurred the wrath of my British superiors. The acts of compliance and obsequiousness required by many British officers hampered me and sometimes even prevented me from fulfilling my responsibility to my men.

My independent manner often had me labeled as a troublemaker. My duty, as I saw it, was to fight for my men's parity with the British soldiers for food, supplies, clothing and arms. I resented the British military policy that treated colonials like second-class subjects. The British refused to give us equal pay, rations and privileges as British soldiers of similar rank. Their discriminatory attitude heightened my budding anti-British sentiments.

One of the defining qualities of leadership is patience. I kept the faith that my vision would come true some day.

Another quality is perseverance. I determined to continually persist until that glorious day came true.

During my presidency, I created an atmosphere conducive to business. With the assistance of the brilliant Alexander Hamilton, my appointee as Secretary of the Treasury, I established economic precedents that enabled the United States to become the world's premier power. We envisioned the United States as becoming the greatest industrial power in the world. We arranged to pay all our debts both state and federal owed by the Continental Congress. We also established the first National Bank.

We tried but failed to get Congress to create centers of manufacturing throughout the entire country. Secretary Hamilton's "Report on Manufacturing" suggested that the federal government should fund industry and act as a catalyst for economic growth due to the absence of private capital. Only Paterson, New Jersey, was actually developed.

In my first administration as President, I outlined the rights and privileges necessary for economic progress such as: protection of private property, free competition, financial responsibility, and a "laissez faire" attitude of government toward commerce. For example, here's my opinion on price controls. In a letter to James Warren in March of 1779, I wrote, "To limit the price of articles is inconsistent with the very nature of things and is impracticable in itself."

I limited bureaucratic restrictions on commerce thus giving it wings to soar. I led in the transformation from the old English system of monopolistic government of favors and privileges into an entirely new, capitalistic form based on merit. My policies, particularly those advocated and pushed through Congress by Federalists, helped create the basis of our economic system. While not perfect, it was far superior to other economic systems.

My farming experiences taught me that as a seed must take root to grow strong; our fledgling nation needed time to blossom to maturity. Our people must learn to appreciate the great style of government they enjoyed. I estimated we needed at least 20 years of peace to grow strong. My "Neutrality Proclamation of 1793" ensured the needed time for the United States to develop. We must be able to successfully resist aggression by any foreign power. It was fortunate that we were able to prevent a war until 1812.

In my annual address to Congress on December 3, 1793, I wrote, "There is no resource so firm for the government of the United States as the affections of the people guided by an enlightened policy." Throughout my life, my vision of America set our direction. Because it was in their own best interest the people followed my lead.

My final advice to America was delivered in my Farewell Address that advocated a "government of as much vigor as is consistent with the perfect security of liberty is indispensable." My political tolerance was expressed to Lafayette from Mount Vernon on Christmas Day 1798: "I think that every nation has a right to establish that form of government under which it conceives it shall live most happy, provided it infracts no right or is not dangerous to others."

John F. Kennedy said this about unimaginative leaders, "Conformity is the jailer of freedom and the enemy of growth." Washington had imagination in abundance. He envisioned thirteen colonies on the fringe of civilization becoming the premier nation in the world. He made his vision come true.

Washington's carefully developed intuition enabled him to see things others could not, or at least, he saw them first.

Being proactive to change often means moving forward before others even know what is happening. In 1793, America was sharply divided between those favoring either Great Britain or France. Washington carefully evaluated the situation, and his analysis guided him to take the action of issuing a Neutrality Proclamation.

Taking no action is sometimes the best action. Washington had learned his lesson well in the Revolutionary

War. From June 1778 at Monmouth until to October 1781 at Yorktown, Washington did not fight a single major battle. When the British challenged him, he refused contact and kept his army intact.

What are the competencies needed by effective leaders? They include being able to influence others, providing team guidance, and flexibility in responding to change, as well as a passion for excellent performance.

Jim Collins, author of *From Good to Great* wrote, "Focusing on what you do best is the only way to greatness." On the need for senior executives to recognize change, Einstein said, "Insanity is doing the same thing over and over and expecting different results."

Tom Peters, well-known business guru, says that leadership is influencing others to greater heights of achievement.

Management guru, Warren Bennis, describes leadership as the "capacity to translate vision into reality" To lead others one must manage oneself.

The effective leader is enthusiastic about his vision. His vision is supported by a worthwhile idea that will benefit others. The vision itself must be clear but its details can be blurry. He passionately promotes his vision. He starts the ball rolling toward vision fulfillment. He persists until he makes his vision a reality. He is proud of his vision and enrolls others. He thinks positively. He makes decisions. He takes action. He gets results. To help him fulfill his vision, he makes emotional appeals to his followers.

Modern visionary leaders who emulate Washington get results. Consider the remarkable history of Apple Computers. Steve Jobs had helped start Apple in 1976 and took it public in 1980 with a 15 % share of America's computer market. Jobs then appointed John Scully as president. Sadly, Jobs got forced out later—supposedly for the good of Apple. Instead of prospering, Apple fell from the tree of computer profitability. Sales were down to only 3.4% of the computer market and

Apple was losing money every day. There was a long-standing lawsuit against Microsoft for patent infringement that was tied up in court. The impasse was stifling creativity within Apple and the company was in dire straits. The hemorrhaging had to be stopped. The Apple Board of Directors re-hired Jobs to take the helm again as CEO.

Jobs immediately demonstrated extraordinary leadership. He settled the lawsuit by going directly to Bill Gates, archenemy of Apple. He suggested that Apple and Microsoft should work together instead of butting heads over a lawsuit. Gates agreed and Jobs dropped the lawsuit.

Jobs breathed life back into Apple by asking for and getting a $150-million infusion of cash from Microsoft in exchange for shares of non-voting stock. At the next stockholder meeting—when he reported what he had done—he was booed for what appeared to be a sellout to Microsoft. Jobs had made a brilliant long-term creative move; he had insured the survival of Apple.

Steve Jobs said this about leaders, "Innovation distinguishes between a leader and a follower." He proved the wisdom of his words by his overture to Gates.

Henry Ford said it was dumb to learn solely from our own experiences. He contended that—by the time we do—we're either too old or too dead to profit by it.

Tom Watson of IBM said, "Nothing so conclusively proves a man's ability to lead others as what he does from day to day to lead himself."

One becomes an effective leader by helping his people develop their own leadership skills. He encourages them to speak out and to take action without fear of punishment for failure or error. Executives who create fearful environments sacrifice many valuable ideas which are never expressed. Subordinates are afraid to speak out for fear of ridicule, punishment, resentment or loss of job. Many leave the company.

The U.S. Marines issue this challenge to leaders:

Stretch your followers to make them rise to their fullest potential. If you tell people you expect only their best from them, that's what you'll get.

After World War II, the military branches debated about what would be the best future recruitment process. The Army, Air Force and Navy opted to make life easier for their new recruits. The Marines adopted the reverse strategy. They decided to make it tougher, so that those who did succeed would be very proud of themselves. The outcome was that the Marines had the highest recruitment. They shared their vision and mission with their recruits, provided direction, showed they cared for the safety of the recruits, and helped them realize their highest aspirations.

The Enron debacle was an example of poor leadership. Integrity was not ingrained within the company culture. With challenges and perceived opportunities, some of Enron's high-level executives proceeded down the slippery slope of unethical and illegal behavior. In their arrogance, they assumed that legal, ethical and moral rules did not apply to them. They could not or would not see what was happening within the company.

Enron's CEO Ken Lay failed in his role. He violated a commandment expressed by Warren Buffett, "Leaders must take action to not only act properly themselves but to enforce ethical conduct by their followers." These principles include trustworthiness, integrity, truth, fairness, compassion, honesty, morality, vision, mission and respect for human dignity.

Stephen Covey wrote, "I am personally convinced that one person can be a change catalyst, a 'transformer' in any situation in any organization, such an individual is the yeast that leavens an entire loaf. It requires vision, initiative, patience, respect, persistence, courage and faith to be a transforming leader."

Stephen Covey, who also wrote the best-selling book, *The Seven Habits of Highly Successful People,* stated that, by using these principles, you can become up to 500% more effective yourself. All modern business experts such as Drucker, Collins, Welch, and Bennis, state that only ethical behavior leads to permanent long-term success.

Think carefully before criticizing. Criticism hurts a person's confidence and damages your relationship with that person. Criticism limits his future contribution to your joint vision. In some cases, the mistake may even be your fault. Perhaps you didn't educate that person fully or properly as to his duties and responsibilities.

George Washington the Surveyor

Chapter Two – Building Character

Noah Webster, the father of the American dictionary, defines character as "a distinctive trait, quality or attribute, an essential quality, moral constitution, moral strength, self-discipline, fortitude, reputation." Webster was a personal friend of George Washington and visited Mount Vernon on several occasions.

Washington wrote his young nephew, George Steptoe Washington, on Dec 5, 1790, concerning his opinion on character: "Good moral character is the first essential in a man."

Thomas Jefferson appraised Washington's character thusly: "He was incapable of fear, meeting personal dangers with the calmest unconcern. Perhaps the strongest feature in his character was prudence, never acting until every circumstance, every consideration was maturely weighed. His integrity was most pure, his justice the most inflexible I have ever known, no motives of interest or consanguinity or friendship, or hatred, being able to bias his decision. He was, indeed, in every sense of the word, a wise, a good and a great man."

President John Adams in his inaugural address as America's second president said that Washington was, "A man who by his long list of great actions regulated by prudence, justice, temperance and fortitude, had merited the gratitude of his fellow citizens, commanded the highest praise of foreign nations and secured immortal glory with posterity."

Robert Hunter, a British visitor to Mount. Vernon, who greatly respected Washington, wrote on 16 November 1785, "Indeed, his greatest pride now is to be thought the first farmer in America. He's quite a Cincinnatus, and often works with the men himself, strips off his coat and labours like a common man."

Not long after the signing of the Jay Treaty on November 10, 1794, ending 30 years of strife between the two countries, former Chief Justice of the Supreme Court John Jay wrote from England, "The best disposition toward us prevails. Next to the King, our president is more popular in this country than any other man in it."

Washington received high praise in January 1778 from another champion of freedom, the Marquis de Lafayette: "Our general is a man truly made for the revolution, which could not be successfully accomplished without him. I see him more closely than any man in the world and I see that he is worthy of the adoration of his country, I admire him more each day for the beauty of his character and his soul."

Benjamin West, the American friend and artist of King George III of England, formerly Washington's most bitter enemy, reported that the king, upon hearing of Washington's resignation as Commander-in-Chief had exclaimed, "That act of closing and finishing what had gone before and viewed in connection with it, placed him in a light the most distinguished of any man living, and that he thought him the greatest character of the age."

Good character is just as vital today among our leaders as it was then. Here is what some modern day business gurus say about the value of good character:

- W. Edwards Deming wrote, "It is not enough to do your best; you must know what to do and then do your best."
- According to Stephen Covey, "Our character is basically a composite of our habits. Because they are consistent, often an unconscious pattern, they constantly, daily express our habits."
- Thomas J. Watson, founder of IBM, said, "If you want to achieve excellence you can get there today. As of this second, quit doing less than excellent work."
- Peter Drucker wrote, "Rank does not confer privilege or power, it imposes responsibility."
- Sam Piazza, CEO of Price Waterhouse, said it succinctly, "It has become dramatically clear that the foundation of corporate integrity is personal integrity."
- Senator Alan Simpson is quoted as saying, "If you have integrity, nothing else matters, if you don't have integrity, nothing else matters."

A person of excellent character exemplifies the highest ethical principles. One with ingrained character finds it easy to make decisions of right and wrong.

Honesty is the Only Policy

Washington wrote in his "circular to the states" on June 8, 1783, "Honesty will be found on every experiment, to be the best and only true policy."

Ambition to do good for others is a worthy character trait. Thomas Jefferson wrote this about Washington, "The moderation and virtue of a single character probably prevented the revolution from being closed, as most others have been, by a subversion of the liberties it intended to establish."

Washington possessed a complex character, strong discipline, an iron will, social, military and political acumen, grace, passion, intelligence and great ambition—all supported by a powerful ego. His ambition to earn the respect of others strengthened his resolve so that he performed seemingly superhuman feats.

Thomas Paine wrote of Washington's retreat from New York in the fall of 1776: "There is a natural firmness in some minds which cannot be unlocked by trifles, but which, when unlocked, discover a cabinet of fortitude, and I reckon it among those kinds of public blessings which we do not immediately see that God hath blessed him with uninterrupted health, and given him a mind that can even flourish upon care."

Our founding fathers established a government based on time-honored ethical principles.

Andrew Carnegie said, "A business is seldom, if ever, built up except on lines of the strictest integrity." Adam Smith believed, "What can be added to the happiness of a man who is in health, out of debt, and has a clear conscience?"

Has "business ethics" become an oxymoron? The American public believes that many leaders today—both in business and politics—are blurring the line between legality and corruption. Being ethical is more than just being legal. People of poor character look for—and often find—loopholes to do wrong. "One needs to put welfare of community above mere profits," said Teddy Roosevelt.

In life we continually encounter stimuli. Then we take an interval—it could be a moment or forever—to fashion a response. Our character determines our response, and that response makes all the difference in world.

American prosperity depends upon our citizens acting ethically and respectfully toward each other. Institutions—be they governments, businesses or families—reflect the character of the people who run them.

George Washington speaks:

I determined in my teen years that I would always do the right thing. I was living with my older half brother, Lawrence, at Mount Vernon, when I encountered a book that had a great influence on me. It was called "The One Hundred Ten Rules of Civility and Decent Behavior in Company and Conversation." It was a 16th century manual written by the Jesuits expressly for the education of young French noblemen.

The first rule was, "Let every action in company be done with a sign of respect to all those present." The last said, "Labor to keep alive in your breast that little spark of celestial fire called conscience."

These two rules typify the content of the entire book—which was how to conduct oneself properly in public. My knowledge of this book helped to foster an excellent relationship with the French officers who came over to help us in our Revolution. It served as my guide for my entire life.

The Second Continental Congress unanimously elected me as Commander-in-Chief of the Continental Army because my fellow delegates trusted me. I refused a salary and decided to serve only for expenses. I did not want the people to think I was serving for money. I felt that I was performing my patriotic duty. Even though the war lasted much longer than I had expected, I did not try to re-negotiate the terms of my contract.

I carried these expenses for over eight years, and I did not ask for any re-imbursement until the war was won. I submitted my expense report as I tendered my resignation to Congress, which audited the report and found it to be accurate.

If we had failed in our quest for independence, I would never have been paid for my expenses. If we had lost the war, the expense money would have been meaningless anyway. King George would have appropriated all my property—including my beloved Mount Vernon—as a traitor to the Crown. That would not have mattered so much to me, for I would have lost my head! Martha would have suffered though.

During my 16 years of patriotic service to the people

(over eight years as General and eight years as President), I lost half of my net worth, as I could not attend properly to my many business interests.

In December 1776—one of the darkest periods in our history—the Continental Congress gave me almost unlimited power. They trusted me to use that power wisely. The American people were fighting a foreign tyrant—King George III—and certainly did not want to have a home grown one! As I wrote to the President of Congress, John Hancock, on Dec 20 1776, "I have no lust for power.

After we had won the war, I resigned my commission as Commander-in- Chief of the Army, the most powerful position in America. It was important that the American people learned to govern themselves. I had refused during the war to become a King or to be made a dictator. Later, I refused a third term as president because I wanted the people to freely vote for my successor.

Because I felt that moral character was the cornerstone for a happy life, I informed my soldiers in General Orders of 2 October 1778, that purity of morals is the only sure foundation of public happiness in any country. As general, I refused to accept special favors fearing that any resulting resentment might create a wall of separation between the soldiers and me. For example, until the men could build wooden huts, I felt duty bound to live in a tent and suffer the indignities of that wretched winter at Valley Forge.

Late in the war, a Tory matron sent Martha (who had been ill) a basket of delicacies. As much as it pained me, I would not let her accept it, for it may have been perceived as accepting favors from the enemy. As the British vacated Boston in March 1776, I issued orders that all Tory property be turned over to the Quartermaster. During this period, my men presented me with a beautiful horse. When I learned that its former owner was a Tory, I turned it in.

On the first of April, 1789, I wrote to General Knox, telling him of the role I intended to assume as President,

"Integrity and firmness is all I can promise: these, be the voyage long or short, never shall forsake me although I may be deserted by all men."

As one of the last acts of his life, Benjamin Franklin bequeathed his crabapple walking stick topped by a golden cap of liberty to me, with these words, "To my friend, and the friend of mankind General Washington, if it were a scepter, he had merited it and would become it."

While on my journey from Mount Vernon to New York City to be inaugurated as the first President, I was offered a very kind toast at a celebration dinner in Baltimore, Maryland: "We behold an example rare in the annals of mankind... a free and enlightened people choosing in a free election without any dissenting vote, the late Commander-in-Chief of the Armies, to watch over and guarantee their civil rights and privileges."

As President—when appointing subordinates—I looked first at a man's character. This was my 'firm' policy: "In every nomination to office, I have endeavored as far as my own knowledge extended or information could be obtained, to make fitness of character my primary object."

I appointed to my first Cabinet men of impeccable character as well as proven ability. Alexander Hamilton as Secretary of Treasury; Thomas Jefferson as Secretary of State; Henry Knox as Secretary of War; and Edmund Randolph as Attorney General were among my first appointments. I nominated John Jay to become the first Chief Justice of the Supreme Court.

I would not let the American people suffer from either cronyism or nepotism. When my young nephew, George Steptoe, asked me to appoint him as a judge in Virginia, I refused saying that he was not as well qualified as others. Furthermore, if I appointed him, I might be censured for showing favoritism. Several years later, however, he was appointed Supreme Court Justice by President Adams. He served the nation well for many years, by helping to write many important decisions.

In my letter to John Posey from army headquarters in Newburgh, New York, on August 7, 1782, I pointed out the contrast between greedy American profiteers and speculators and my Continental soldiers. The former were becoming obscenely rich, while the latter suffered incredible hardships. Profiteers acted unconscionably—during the same time that their fellow countrymen were sacrificing and suffering in the fight to win independence for all.

I wrote Posey, "Conscience seldom comes to a man's aid while he is in the zenith of health and reveling in pomp and luxury upon ill-gotten gains. It is generally the last act of his life and comes too late to be of much service to others here, or to himself hereafter."

George Washington with his Horse

Integrity as a Corporate Culture

There are a number of contemporary business leaders who put the interests of the public first. Herb Kelleher, a character with character, is one of the best examples.

It has been said of Herb Kelleher that—during his tenure as CEO of Southwest—his colorful personality created a corporate culture which made Southwest employees well-known for taking themselves lightly but their jobs seriously. Southwest is consistently named among the top five Most Admired Corporations in America in *Fortune* magazine's annual poll. *Fortune* has also called him perhaps the best CEO in America.

In the 1970s, practicing lawyer Kelleher joined with established businessman, Rollin King, to form Southwest Airlines. They sought to provide a service that travelers wanted—a short-haul, no-frills and low-cost airline. He took the trouble to listen to potential customers to determine what they most wanted in the aviation marketplace. Once he learned their desires, he took radical actions to make their wishes a reality.

Kelleher went against the conventional wisdom. He would have only one class of airplane—the 737. He used airports in small towns to keep costs low. Instead of following the failed methods of other airlines for loading and unloading people and baggage and servicing planes for turnaround, he acted innovatively by adapting stock car racing pit techniques used at the track for his system. Other airlines at the time were looking inward to make small adjustments by fine-tuning their operations. Kelleher made gigantic innovative leaps by transformational leadership.

Herb Kelleher is a master communicator. He relayed important messages in a clear and understandable way. He also listened attentively to everyone, both high and low. He exhibited a powerful presence. He was out there among his people. They knew him and he knew them. They knew what he stood for and what he expected from them. By being out among them—and not walled up in the corner office—he learned at first hand of both opportunities and problems.

Kelleher would pitch in with routine duties such as handling luggage, passing out peanuts, taking reservations, and picking up trash. Herb Kelleher set the example that everyone should do whatever was necessary, regardless of his or her position within the company. He also encouraged the application of ethical principles by encouraging employees to "let every action in company be done with a sign of respect to all those present."

Southwest Airlines people clearly enjoyed doing their jobs. Feeling good about themselves and their company resulted in better service to the customers. Kelleher settled a trademark dispute with another airline by offering to arm wrestle its CEO. This prevented rancor from developing between the two companies, saved on legal bills, and brought a sense of humor into an otherwise tense business situation.

Southwest Airlines established a Cultural Committee of 70 people, whose job it was to determine first how best to serve the community. The company then implemented the recommended actions to do just that. The result was to provide a caring atmosphere for servicing the needs of passengers. In turn, the company received support from the public and ticket sales increased.

In 2006, the International Air Transport Association reported that Southwest was the largest airline in the United States by number of passengers carried domestically for any one year and the second largest airline in the world by number of passengers carried. It also maintains the fourth-largest fleet of aircraft among all of the world's commercial airlines. Southwest Airlines provides benefits for most of its stakeholders. This great company reflects the character of its leader.

On the other hand, Enron had a printed "Code of Ethics," but it was not adhered to because it wasn't ingrained in Enron's corporate culture. Enron is a warning of what happens when unethical behavior consumes a company.

Enron had been a $70 billion-dollar corporation, whose stock sold at $80 dollars a share. When the bubble burst, all of its stakeholders—employees, shareholders, customers, lenders, lawyers, accountants—were injured. The principle of greed ruled this corporate culture and destruction was the outcome.

The Enron story is one of greed, lies, scandal, heartbreak, and revenge. All of American business was tainted by its example.

George Washington speaks:

After 1763, during the years leading up to Revolutionary War the British intensified what many Americans felt was an unfair, even blatant, disregard for their rights. We felt that, even though we were born in America, we were Englishmen with the same rights as those born in the homeland.

I argued unsuccessfully with the British for years for equal rights but finally concluded that total independence would be our only escape from their tyranny. Thereafter, I did not take small tentative steps to adjust the existing system, but instead opted to establish an entirely new form of government. To make this possible, I took the responsibility for leading the Continental Army. We were on the field of battle for over eight years under the most difficult conditions—but we prevailed.

Washington was always out among his troops. He was not one to sit in the office. He "led by walking around." He did so even during the many miserably cold winters of the War. The suffering men—seeing him among them—knew he was not back at headquarters warming his hindquarters before the fire. He shared in the men's hardships and conversed with them to know their problems and their needs in order to best solve them. At the battle of Princeton in January, 1777, he was up front urging them, "Come on, boys, it's a fine day for a fox hunt!"

Washington was humble and did not consider himself above performing even the most mundane acts. While marching to Trenton on an icy Christmas night in 1776, he saw a cannon stuck in a steep ravine along a creek bed. Washington got off his horse, put his shoulder to the cannon wheel, and pushed it free. Seeing this, the men cheered and the word spread. Later, at the second battle of Trenton, Washington stayed astride his horse on a bridge as his men rushed across to safety even as British shells were bursting all around them. He felt that his men benefited from his calm presence amidst the greatest danger. He was the last one leaving Brooklyn on the earlier escape from Long Island and last in line nearest the enemy during the retreat across New Jersey.

Washington arose early each day before the crack of dawn to write daily General Orders to the soldiers. To make sure the men were fully informed, he also made personal emotional appeals to them, talked informally and formally with them, and held briefings at mid-day mess. Great communicators listen attentively and respectfully to the speakers. Washington welcomed all sources of information.

George Washington speaks:

I remember the day shortly before my 6th birthday, when my father called, "George, come into the parlor with me. Please sit down. Let's have a man-to-man talk. You're a good son. Your mother and I are proud of you. Naturally, we want you to have a happy and prosperous life. It's my responsibility to start teaching you the ethical and moral principles of life."

"Have you learned the seventh commandment from the Bible? The one that says, 'Thou shall not bear false witness?' Do you know what that means? My boy, it means to never tell a lie."

"Yes, Poppa", I replied

"Let's make a Father Son Agreement. I promise to never lie to you. Now you promise me that you will always tell the truth. Will you promise?"

"Yes, Poppa, I promise I will never tell a lie"

A few months later, I got a hatchet for my birthday. I had seen adults use hatchets to cut down trees so I thought I could follow their example. Therefore, I went around Mount

Vernon finding things to chop, and then one day I chopped down the cherry tree.

My father was very angry when he discovered his beloved cherry tree on the ground. Then he saw me standing over in the corner with my hatchet in my hand.

He asked me politely, "George, did you chop down my cherry tree?"

My stomach knotted up. I felt sick. How should I answer? Then I remembered my promise to him and stammered, "Yes, Poppa, I can not tell a lie. I did chop down your cherry tree?"

Did he punish me for my act? No! His face beamed as he spread his arms out wide and said, "Fly into my arms, my dear son. I am so proud of you for you having told me the truth."

I have never forgotten that day. I learned valuable lessons that have served me well throughout my life. I chose to tell the truth and that has made all the difference in the world to me.

My contemporary, the poet Alexander Pope, wrote in his Essay on Man in 1734 about how childhood experiences influence our future character: "Just as the twig is bent, the tree's inclined."

Later in life, when I was leading men, I realized that they too might feel ill at ease from being thrust into new circumstances. I treated them with respect and compassion to make them feel comfortable. As I had not known right from wrong as a youngster, my new men did not always know their duties. It was my responsibility to teach them. This was particularly important as Commander-in-Chief of the Continental Army, for most of my soldiers were teenagers just off the farm.

As my father had done with me, I set an example for my men. I would always act to earn their trust, and I expected the same from them. This meant more than just telling the truth. As they went about their work, if they made a mistake, I thought twice before punishing them. Perhaps it was my fault for not properly informing them?

If a man made a mistake, I kept my emotions in check. If I got angry with anyone, I did not show it unless for purposes of good effect. I first asked questions to learn the true and full facts about all situations. When my men performed properly, I praised and rewarded them. Honest mistakes I forgave. Intentional wrongdoing I punished. My primary concern was not to blame but to solve problems.

On December 26, 1799, twelve days after Washington's death, a Joint Assembly of Congress was held in the nation's capital, Philadelphia. There, "Light Horse Harry" Lee, who had been Washington's cavalry commander in the Revolutionary War, read the eulogy written by John Marshall—then a Congressman but later the Chief Justice of the Supreme Court. It is a most fitting character tribute that rings true even today: "First in War, First in Peace and First in the hearts of his countrymen, second to none in humble and enduring scenes of private life; Pious, just, humane, temperate and sincere; uniform, dignified and commanding; his example was as edifying to all around him as were the effects of that example lasting. Correct throughout, vice shuddered in his presence and virtue always felt his fostering hand. The purity of his private character gave effulgence to his public virtues."

Both George Washington and Herb Kelleher portrayed a depth of character that was consistent with their core values. They treated all people with respect. They sought out people of similar character to serve with them.

George Washington Crossing the Delaware River

Chapter Three – Calculating Risk

The same risk management techniques that Washington used to evaluate risks in all his business and government service can be used by today's business leaders. Higher or lower productivity is a direct result of a company's risk/reward relationship. The worst-case scenario is for a company to go out of business. At the very least, the risk is to under-utilize resources—which lowers productivity.

George Washington speaks:

By mid-December 1776, only five months after the Declaration of Independence had been signed, it seemed as though our fight for freedom was all but lost. The overwhelmingly powerful British Army had repeatedly beaten us in New York, and then had driven us from pillar to post all across New Jersey. Now we were on the Pennsylvania side of the Delaware River. The British and their hired mercenaries, the Hessians, were camped just across the river—very close to our capital, Philadelphia.

During this ordeal of fighting and retreating, we had lost nearly 90% of our army plus most of our cannon, ammunition, winter clothes, and tents—and much of everything else that soldiers need. Despair had gripped my soldiers. Their enlistments would expire in about two weeks on January 1, 1777.

As I walked among them, I heard many of them say that they could hardly wait to go home. If they left, then our cause was lost. We would have no army. The existence of our Continental Army was all that gave legitimacy to our struggle for independence. I had to keep it in the field!

Panic had also spread throughout our citizenry. Many had signed oaths of re-allegiance to the King. These were the blackest of days. Thomas Paine, who accompanied our army as it retreated, wrote the "The American Crisis," at night while seated at the campfire. It begins with these immortal words, "these are the times that try men's souls."

If we sat idle here on the Pennsylvania shore or retreat further west, we would be safe—but only temporarily. The British would again pursue us in the spring. I refused to let the flame of freedom flicker out. We must strike a blow against them to boost our morale—but where, when and how?

Fortunately for us, in early December the British and their Hessian mercenaries decided to go into winter quarters. This was normal procedure for European armies. They established isolated outposts all across New Jersey to subjugate the citizens. One outpost, manned by their Hessian mercenaries, was at Trenton just across the river from us.

This presented a potential target too good to resist. It was relatively weakly manned by about 1200 soldiers. I gathered my staff and we discussed the risks of attacking there. Normally we would not risk all on one venture but here we had no choice. We were in a do or die situation. We adopted the code "Victory or Death."

For the Trenton attack I early engaged a double agent, John Honeyman, who informed us of the enemy territory that we would invade—physically, mentally and emotionally. If we did nothing and remained on the safe side of the Delaware River, we would severely jeopardize the success of our glorious cause. Playing it safe would cost us everything. Attacking would be risky, but could lead to fulfilling our mission.

Our goal remained the same throughout the war: we were determined to drive the British from our shores and make them grant us independence. But it would be well nigh impossible to drive them out in one fell swoop. We had tried that earlier at Brooklyn with disastrous results. Here at Trenton, we could strike a limited blow at the enemy's weakest point.

We decided to take everything we had across the river and attack Trenton at dawn the morning after Christmas. We did so and won a resounding victory. Not one of our men was killed in battle, but two of our soldiers froze to death en route. Our four wounded included 19-year-old Lt. James Monroe, later to become our Fifth President. We killed or wounded about 200 of the enemy, captured about 950 and the rest were able to run away in the confusion.

A week later, we fought the Second Battle of Trenton. Just when they thought they had us trapped, we slipped away around them in the middle of the night to soundly defeat their forces left behind at Princeton that next morning. In the space of less than two weeks, we had severely damaged the morale of the enemy. In the ensuing ten-week period, we broke their hold on New Jersey, and ruined their strategy of continually subjecting our citizens to tyranny.

During this period, the entire mood of the war was reversed. The British attitude changed from feeling invincible to defeatist. Having lost their confidence, they felt they couldn't win. We Americans changed from a feeling of utter hopelessness to the belief that we could not lose.

One of the keys to our ultimate victory in the

Revolutionary War was the difference in leadership principles between them and us. The British and Hessian leadership remained rigid and hierarchical. Their men in charge dictated all their actions. I operated under an open and flexible system that contributed to our ultimate success. We would plan and prepare together. In a letter to a friend I wrote, "Only desperate men leap before they look." We were desperate to be sure but I kept my wits about me. I always carefully analyzed the various possibilities that lay before us.

I never mimicked the enemy by doing as he did. I was proactive and did what he least expected. In those days, European armies normally went into winter quarters and would not fight again until spring. Fighting in winter was too difficult. There would be no grazing for the horses, and the roads would be icy and hazardous.

Here, across the river from Trenton I did not go into winter quarters. I misled the Hessian commander, Colonel Rall, through my double agent, to think that I would do so. Fortunately, Rall thought that Honeyman was his man. I had told Honeyman to inform Rall that we were demoralized and planning to go into winter quarters soon. Rall believed Honeyman that we could not hurt a flea—as evidenced by our continually retreating.

Although various contingents of the Continental Army were separated over many miles, I didn't wait to gather them in. When I felt that the moment was right—which actually occurred on Christmas night—I would attack with all the strength at my disposal. If Rall caught us out on the river while crossing over, the result could be catastrophic for us. On the other hand, if we were caught in open countryside the British and Hessians could trap us. After figuratively lulling Rall to sleep, I pounced upon him, taking all my men and cannon.

I took careful preliminary precautions to lessen the risk. I chose a crossing seven miles up the river—the more likely to escape notice by the Hessians. I sent a small force over to the New Jersey side of the river crossing point early on the day of the attack to arrest all civilians and muzzle all dogs to keep the silence. Despite these precautions, a Tory did see us and went to Rall to tell him we were coming. Rall completely ignored the warning. His negligence not only cost him his command but also his life later that same morning.

The Delaware River had been an obstacle. We had turned it into an opportunity. Before we had attacked Trenton, I had made use of this time to create an effective organization.

When we were ready, I made the army the driver of events by attacking. We would not wait idly to be driven. Although I made my men part of the planning and preparation process, I reserved for myself the final decision. I realized that progress or change always engenders risk. Nothing can be gained without it. Seeking progress means abandoning a safe status quo. Only by putting ourselves in harm's way at Trenton could we strike a blow for ultimate victory.

I made it a rule to carefully analyze all aspects of the enemy's situation. I then accommodated myself to take advantage of it. If the enemy's strength was overpowering, I would not attack. If the enemy was weak and vulnerable, then I would do so. Trenton, Princeton, Germantown and Yorktown are the best examples of our taking the initiative.

Before embarking at Trenton, I inspired the men by reminding them of our glorious cause. Our action today would be a most important step. Our future as free men hinged on what would happen this very night. I told the men that once we embarked there could be no turning back.

In the midst of loading the boats the weather turned much worse. The temperature, which was already below freezing, dropped steadily. Ice was forming everywhere—in the boats and on the docks. Conditions could not have been more miserable. It took much longer than I had expected to load the cannon and horses, so we didn't get across until about 4:00 o'clock in the morning. We had lost two hours! We could not possibly get to Trenton until after daybreak, thus losing the advantage of a dawn attack.

As we disembarked on the enemy's territory I dared not halt or delay in making decisions. I kept the men going forward, with only limited short breaks. I divided the army into two columns which would converge as they reached Trenton—thus partially encircling the town. Dividing your army in enemy territory is very risky. Nevertheless, the result of this risk turned out to be a Godsend for us.

We won a glorious victory at Trenton. A few days later, I addressed the men and begged them to reenlist. I told them that they would never again have such an opportunity to serve their country. Fortunately, enough men reenlisted to keep our Army intact.

I took the Army on to Princeton and again defeated the British. After these extended moves, I thought it a good idea to tighten up and re-evaluate our present situation before proceeding further. I discussed with my staff the question of whether to go farther or retreat to safety? We all agreed that, in this case, discretion was the better part of valor.

I did not lead them on to Brunswick where the British kept their war chest. Capturing all their money perhaps could have possibly won the war for us immediately, but why reach out too far and risk it all? Getting there and then having to protect the money from British recapture would have exhausted the men beyond endurance. They would have been defenseless. The men had performed magnificently and they deserved a rest—which is why I led them to winter camp at Morristown, New Jersey.

Our results for this ten-day period were better than we had dreamed. Our out-maneuvering and out-fighting the British shocked them into a state of utter frustration. That is a principle for risk management. Protect your people from exhaustion and burnout. Inflict that pain upon your enemy.

At our winter camp in Morristown, I made good use of superior positioning. It was located near the main line of British communication from New York to Philadelphia. We could hang on their flank and impede their ease of movement.

Furthermore, it also had an excellent natural defensive range of hills. We would send out raiding parties to harass the British. Then, when we were chased, we could retreat into the shelter of our defenses.

George Washington and His Artillery

Here is another example of greed overcoming sound risk reward ratios. Back in the mid to late 1980s the investment firm of Prudential Bache was found guilty of selling fraudulent tax shelters. As a result, the federal government fined them a billion dollars. In addition, the company had to reimburse the customers for their losses. Those costs drove the company out of business. They had gone overboard in recommending too many risky investments to the public.

The other brokerage firms would have been wise to have gone after Prudential Bache's disgruntled customers. They could have capitalized on the negative publicity surrounding those illegal acts. Some did.

CEOs, therefore, are obligated to carefully analyze every factor before making a decision. Even a decision to do nothing is a decision. While the effective leader must be optimistic, he must never underestimate the risks. He can't be too pessimistic either for he might never take a risk. Leaders must, therefore, work to develop rational emotional intelligence skills to evaluate risk properly.

Effective leaders develop a strategy, but must keep it flexible enough to take advantage of unforeseen circumstances. CEOs must constantly re-evaluate the ever-changing competitive market conditions. Before venturing into unknown territory one should obtain as much knowledge as possible, in other words, hire a spy. Knowing the territory helps to avoid unpleasant surprises.

Leaders learn to evaluate risk/reward outcomes by using several methods. One is book knowledge. Another is by analyzing the experiences of others. Most important, however, is a careful reflection of one's own experiences. Questions one must ask oneself are "Am I taking a big risk for a small potential reward?" Or conversely, "Would it be equally foolish for me to pass up the potential for a big reward for a relatively small risk?"

A business must incur risk in order to succeed. The challenge is managing the risk. Even giant oil companies take on partners to share the risk of drilling a dry hole.

George Washington speaks:

Because of the weakness of the Continental Army, I most often avoided battles with the British. I fought only when the conditions seemed to be in my favor or when fighting was unavoidable. Unavoidable were all the battles in New York and at Brandywine, which we lost. Our cause was my only important consideration. One such occasion was during the most desperate days at Valley Forge. That February of 1778, we were down to only about 3,000 men fit for duty. I listed 15,000 able-bodied men on our rosters.

The British too had spies. I knew I had to keep them fooled. Since the British had roughly 12,000 men in Philadelphia—only a day's march away—I knew they would have attacked us immediately if only they had known the truth. The reverse was also true. When we were strong I listed fewer men to encourage the British to attack us.

Fooling the British, of course, fooled our citizens. Many thought to themselves, "if you're so strong, George Washington, why don't you attack the British and drive them off our soil?" Many of our citizens thought I was either too lazy or cowardly.

Once we had identified an opportunity, selected a strategy, and decided upon tactics to strike, we then took prompt action as we had at Trenton. There is no substitute for action.

At Trenton, I introduced an American ethic of warfare that John Adams later called the "policy of humanity." It proved that moral behavior after a victory could lead to future favorable results. The Battle of Trenton was the first time we had captured enemy soldiers—in this case Hessians. I treated these prisoners humanely. If their comrades still under arms reciprocated in future actions, this would reduce the risk to my men of mistreatment if captured or wounded.

Furthermore, I hoped that many Hessians would desert

and come over to our side. To encourage them, I marched the prisoners through the German villages in Pennsylvania so they see how prosperous their former countrymen were. I knew their impressions would get back to their comrades. European soldiers often "murdered" wounded enemies or those who were trying to surrender, under the rules of warfare then known as giving the enemy "no quarter."

American companies can face a financial risk no matter what decision they make. An auto manufacturer had built a car that later proved to have a dangerous defective part. They could choose to recall all the cars and install a replacement part. That would be very expensive. There was another choice. Their accounting department estimated that the company could pay off a relatively small number of injured party lawsuits and thus save the firm a lot of money. In other words, the company could skip the recall and take their chances of being sued. Fortunately, the company took the high road and recalled saving an untold number of lives and injuries.

An instructive modern-day example of evaluating risk is the story of Lee Iacocca. He assumed the responsibility of resurrecting a failing company, Chrysler. Lee had done good job leading Ford Motor Company. However, Iacocca had crossed swords with owner Henry Ford II, and was summarily dismissed. Iacocca decided to accept the presidency of Chrysler and remain in the auto business.

Iacocca saw Chrysler as a unique opportunity. He could save thousands of jobs for a long-established company and make some money for himself. He could also regain the prestige lost by his recent dismissal.

Chrysler in the early 1980s was on its knees and facing bankruptcy. Employee morale was very low, as they had little hope for the company's future. The company was losing money rapidly. They faced stiff competition from other auto companies who were building better and more appealing cars. The competition also had more advertising, more money, and better employee morale.

If Iacocca could bring Chrysler back to profitability, he would earn the reputation of being a remarkable leader who got outstanding results. He decided to risk his reputation on a massive career gamble.

Iacocca took the job as Chrysler's President for 1$ a year salary and stock options that had a relatively low present value. His financial success would depend completely on what happened to the value of Chrysler's stock. He knew that he was good at the car business and his competence bred self-confidence.

To finance the rejuvenation of Chrysler, Iacocca talked the U.S. Government into loaning him a huge sum of money. He became a showman for Chrysler, accentuating the trend that top executives personally appear on television to advertise their products and services. Iacocca spent a fortune on ads. "If you can find a better car, buy it." He conveyed the message of Chrysler quality repeatedly to potential buyers.

Iacocca's optimistic attitude rubbed off on his employees. He constantly communicated optimism to the employees. They began to believe in themselves and that they could produce a superior product. He made them feel that they were part of a team that would pull the company out of bankruptcy and keep their jobs intact.

Iacocca's strategy worked. Chrysler became known as the symbol of a high-quality product. He became a household name. He made a fortune on his stock appreciation. He had kept an old established company alive. Iacocca is an excellent modern example of risking and winning. Everyone in this venture won.

The worst possible outcome for a company is to go out of business. This hurts all their stakeholders. Companies manage risk by taking measures to become more efficient at managing processes and more effective at leading their people. Here are some case histories of companies, which were once at risk, but improved enough to stay alive in an increasingly competitive global environment. Their leadership made the necessary changes to keep them viable. Productivity guru David Allen states that only 30% of a company's resources are effectively used for production. This means that in the typical business 70% of resources are under-utilized. If that ratio could be reversed, then America would again be on the right track to higher productivity.

Andy Grove, CEO of Intel, faced a major problem back in the mid 1980s. The company was on the verge of bankruptcy. The Japanese—with a new improved version of memory chips—had captured a major share of Intel's business. Grove had underestimated the danger and was not prepared with an alternative strategy. He should have listened to bright young new hires, encouraged rigorous debate, and been more receptive to alternatives.

Effective leaders do not look to assess blame, they look to find solutions. Gordon Moore, co-founder of Intel visited Grove in his office one day during this crisis. Grove asked him, "Suppose we go and a new CEO comes in, what should he do first?" Moore answered, "Get us out of memory chips." Grove replied, "So let's go outside and come back in to do just that."

They did so and started producing microprocessors. It was traumatic at first, but they had no choice. The strategy worked and the company started prospering as never before. Grove learned two valuable lessons: don't ignore the market place, and don't try to impose wishful thinking upon it.

In times of drastic change like these, disgruntled employees can be resentful of change if they do not fully understand its purpose. Therefore, effective leaders constantly communicate to their employees how it is in their own best interest to embrace the change.

Why do so many successful companies in the fast-moving, innovative high tech industry fail? One reason is that the speed of new inventions and processes make the old obsolete very quickly. If a successful, entrenched company has profitable products and service systems out in the market place, then they are reluctant to jeopardize their proven successes to chase the new kid on the block.

New companies with nothing to lose can devote time, energy, and resources to promote innovation. They often leave older companies in the dust. They too—after a few years or even months—can find themselves in the same predicament. The way to minimize this risk is adopt a strategy of constant alertness to spot any change coming down the pike.

Workers closer to the action seem to know more and be aware sooner about changes in the market or technology. Effective leaders are more attentive listeners and can therefore make more intelligent decisions. Executives who closet themselves behind closed doors run great risks of being left behind.

Small entrepreneurial companies are more nimble and can respond more quickly to the marketplace. They do not have an entrenched bureaucracy to inhibit them. They can more quickly implement their entire processes down to completion.

Throughout history, people who were new to or outside a discipline have made major breakthroughs in creative thought. This is largely because they have not learned what supposedly cannot be done.

A Calculated Risk

Johnson & Johnson, makers of Tylenol, had a big scare in a classic case in which a number of customers had died after taking the drug. No one knew why. Johnson and Johnson had the option to deny blame, claiming that their quality control is so rigorously controlled; it could not possibly be their fault. They were facing many lawsuits for actual and punitive damages.

Johnson & Johnson could be found guilty, with judgments large enough to force the company into bankruptcy. Another scenario had sales of Tylenol drying up due to fear by consumers of buying tainted goods. Neither was a winning option.

At a huge financial cost, Tylenol avoided all risk. They reviewed their vision and mission statements that had been inaugurated by their founder, General Johnson, many years before. This code required that the company always put their customers first.

Johnson & Johnson decided to do the ethical and moral thing. They pulled all the Tylenol bottles off the shelves, at a cost of over $100 million. The decision was successful, for no one else got sick or died. The result was that Johnson & Johnson came out with a greatly increased reputation as a "good neighbor" company and that contributed to high profitability. It was later proven that one unbalanced person in one town had tampered with the Tylenol bottles.

George Washington speaks:

During the Revolutionary War, a smallpox epidemic always loomed on the horizon. Smallpox was especially prevalent and deadly. An army could be destroyed from within or so weakened that an enemy could successfully attack. When men get smallpox naturally, there is a 30 to 40% mortality rate. The smallpox death rate from inoculation is low at 1-3% but there is an assumed risk, as healthy men are deliberately infected. I deemed it a necessity to inoculate soldiers and civilians against smallpox. Although the men would be very sick for two to three weeks, at least with inoculations I could stagger the sickness. All the men wouldn't be sick at the same time.

In those days, the doctor took pus from a live victim and put it into an open cut of a healthy person. Consequently, inoculations were illegal in some jurisdictions at the time, and I had to work around that. To those soldiers who objected, I pointed out to them that my beloved Martha—she of the beautiful smooth complexion—had been inoculated.

This shamed the men into compliance. I was immune myself—having had a mild case of smallpox I had contacted in Barbados as a lad of 19 years. By inoculating my men, I undertook a small known risk to avoid a big, potentially disastrous and dangerous one.

Washington at Valley Forge

Chapter Four – Engendering Loyalty

George Washington speaks:

I demonstrated my respect to my troops constantly by word and deed. Therefore, they remained loyal to me under the most trying circumstances. They constantly braved incredible hardships to keep the flame of liberty burning brightly. Continental Army soldiers sacrificed themselves to protect their fellow Americans from British atrocities. In turn, many American civilians, but sadly not all, were patriots and supported the Army.

High morale engenders loyalty. The higher the level of loyalty in any organization the more productive it is. My soldiers were usually hungry, ill clothed, tired and under the constant threat of being overwhelmed by the vastly superior British Army. Men constantly under pressure need periods of rest and relaxation to compose themselves.

I kept their morale high by using every innovative

method I could think of to provide a change of pace for the men. I sponsored plays in the evenings with my soldiers being the actors, often prompting howling delights from their fellow soldiers out in the audience. We would sing at regular songfests, hold dances, and those who could play musical instruments did so for the enjoyment of all. They would also kid each other by taunts and joking around even under the most miserable conditions. One of their favorite greetings, "Good morning, Brother Soldier, and how are ye today?" "Freezing and starving, thank ye and I hope that you are the same."

Jim Collins, author of *From Good to Great* writes that it is neither technology nor charismatic leadership, but the people themselves that create great companies. He believes that leaders who are humble—but with an iron will to succeed—have proven to be the most successful. They encourage their people to think for themselves. They always act in a disciplined manner. Collins' criteria for greatness are rigid. Of the 1,435 companies in his study, only 11 have met his criteria of greatness.

Employees have needs over and above money. Leaders should never overlook providing for human needs such as empathy and fairness. If leaders do not provide these to their followers, they may go elsewhere.

George Washington speaks:

I forgave General Greene for the debacle at Fort Washington in the fall of 1776. He had assured me it was defensible so I had not ordered it evacuated as I had earlier planned. General Greene was too good a man for me to let one error derail his further serving our cause. His loyalty in the battles down South helped insure our independence.

A CEO must maintain a certain level of aloof dignity. CEOs also should never let themselves be seen as stagnant. They should always keep their vision onward and upward.

Change is imperative.

George Washington speaks:

I always had the men in action. Even at Valley Forge, I roused the men at daybreak. They had assigned duties to clean out their huts and police the area. They must stand guard and act as sentries, even though they often had to share clothes with their hut mates to go outside on sentry duty.

Later after General von Steuben's arrival, I had him march the men off their feet every day in a series of various drills. Also bayonet practice. I encouraged the men with a "let's do it together attitude." In many of my reports to the men, I referred to us as a 'band of brothers.'

Would it be fair to treat all my men the same. No! For example, I didn't give good workers more assignments, just because they could and would do it.

I solicited information from everyone. I asked each what they most wanted. What were their dreams for the future? I also was careful to make the men feel comfortable enough to always tell me the truth, even if it were bad news. Open channels of communication build and maintain trust. The great asset within the Continental Army was mutual trust. Trust begets loyalty. The more I knew about the men, the better I could serve them. Together we would make a larger contribution to winning our cause. I sought first to understand them and then be sure they understood me.

President Washington dealt with the difficult question of loyalty with the Neutrality Proclamation. He carefully and painstakingly evaluated the current situation in America. Half the population were pro-British, the other half pro-French. It was in the best interest of America to side with neither. Washington could not let internal dissension flare up into any type of overt action that would favor either side. At first, citizens on both sides were against the Proclamation, but they soon understood its wisdom.

A short definition of increased productivity is to get more output per unit of input. One of the most outstanding examples of productivity in all of American history is the Continental Army. Washington won the most 'ultimate victory' from the least at the beginning—a bunch of farm boy amateur soldiers. Without any doubt the teams of superior performers he developed worked harmoniously together to produce an outstanding result—independence and freedom from tyranny. Pride in organizational accomplishments retains good people.

Today's business leaders—in pushing for more corporate productivity—are often perceived by their employees as merely asking them to work harder. Change is traumatic. It causes angst among the workers. What's in this for me, they ask? They may view it as one-sided—benefiting only the company or even the managers' own personal goals. The CEO must convince them that striving for higher productivity is in their own best interests. Higher productivity means a larger total pie for all to share. If shared fairly, it is of benefit to all stakeholders. Leaders must be very energetic in explaining the benefits until they are understood by all concerned.

The most effective leaders don't need to tell people that they must do a task. They merely note that it must be done. They should be subtle with their followers wording it so that they feel privileged to do it. Effective leaders make it seem like a desire of the work force. Mark Twain was a genius in portraying this skill. He has Tom Sawyer gets his friends to paint his fence for him by making them want too as a privilege they will enjoy. There's a world of difference between demanding that something be done and consenting to have it done.

Common sense tells us that loyal employees are more productive. They pay more attention to their present position and are not thinking about other job possibilities. Companies have to earn loyalty, by minimizing the anxiety of employees worried about job loss through outsourcing and downsizing. To maximize productivity, companies should take the initiative to boost loyalty through building morale. Senior executives can build morale by encouraging employees to feel that they are doing meaningful work, and by treating them in a dignified manner.

Arrogant bosses quickly lose the loyalty of their employees. An example of this was Mr. X of a well-known company. Mr. X had been a big achiever, but lost the loyalty of personnel by treating them like peasants who just happened to live in his own personal fiefdom. Early on his success won for him an Executive of the Year award. But five years later a leading finance magazine labeled him a "case study in negativism."

Mr. X was the victim of his own success. He began to feel invincible, as George III had done during the Revolutionary War. He developed a blindness, or unwillingness or even inability to see the truth. Mr. X felt that the rules of ethical conduct didn't apply to him. His self-conceit smothered his other talents and abilities.

Trust engenders loyalty. Distrust is deadly within any organization—particularly if employees believe that the boss ignores their needs and thinks only of himself. Leaders are not loyal to their employees if they callously disregard their best interests. Loyalty is a two-way street.

George Washington speaks:

The American people went from utter despair to great exultation in the space of the ten-day period from December 26, 1776 to January 4, 1777. From the summer of 1776 our soldiers had been discouraged to the point of utter despair, as was our entire fledgling country. Our soldiers and civilians alike were ready to give up our vision quest for freedom and independence. The British had offered amnesty to all those who would re-swear allegiance to the crown. Many citizens had already signed oaths of re-allegiance to the British and many more planned to, believing that future resistance was hopeless. Our cause appeared lost.

The Continental Army—our only hope for freedom from British tyranny—had been defeated in New York City that summer and fall of 1776 by overwhelmingly superior forces. We were kicked from pillar to post as we retreated all across New Jersey toward Pennsylvania.

Our men were freezing, as they were half-naked, wearing worn out summer clothes. They were hungry. All were miserable. Many had no shoes. You could trace the progress of our army by the bloody footprints left behind on the snow and ice. A large number of our men had been killed or wounded in battle, many others had died from diseases or were very ill, and others had deserted by merely walking home undetected.

We re-crossed the icy Delaware River that Christmas of 1776 to attack the isolated Hessian outpost at Trenton. We won a glorious victory. We accomplished something else that was entirely new for us. We captured a very large number of prisoners. What should we do with them? Many of my soldiers wanted to punish them, even execute them, for the atrocities they had committed upon American citizens—raping, plundering and pillaging our citizens on a massive scale both in New York and as they had pursued us across New Jersey.

According to the rules of war at the time, we could have given them "no quarter" and executed them all. I insisted, however, that we treat these prisoners leniently. It was the compassionate thing to do. As they had surrendered to us, I felt that we were now responsible for their lives. One of the causes we were fighting for was that all men, as human beings, were entitled to be treated with respect and dignity.

Pragmatically, my decision of leniency could also protect my men's lives. I thought that the Hessians, in future battles, would be more apt to surrender than fight us to the death. Furthermore, most of the German soldiers were not here of their own free will. Their rulers had rented them out as mercenaries (and pocketed the rent monies). In future difficult situations, many might desert over to our side. I also hoped that my treatment of the prisoners would entice those Hessians still under arms to follow my example and not massacre our wounded or prisoners.

As victors we were entitled to the "spoils of war." The Hessians had a large supply depot, particularly of shoes—all of which I immediately divided among my men. They also left a war chest of almost $12,000. This was divided among the men as well. I did not participate in this sharing and neither did my officers, who followed my example. European armies did exactly the opposite: their officers took the bulk of the spoils, leaving very little for the rank and file. My decision to let the men share the entire spoils among themselves did wonders to improve loyalty. Their hope for future spoils aided both enlistment and re-enlistments.

After the victory at Trenton, I had planned to attack the British at Princeton—only another nine miles away—that same morning. However, I observed that many of my soldiers were staggering about. I asked a sergeant, "What's the matter with these men?"

"They're drunk, sir,"

"Drunk?"

"Yes, Sir, from overly celebrating our victory."

"How did that happen?"

"They liberated the Hessians store of rum."

"Oh well, the men must have their celebration," I admitted.

Celebrating triumphs boosts loyalty, so we immediately re-embarked on the same boats back over to the Pennsylvania side. Of course, we had to take the Hessian prisoners with us. They were afraid to get into the boats at first, but finally—with some spirited cajoling by our men—they cooperated. As we crossed over, we beat our feet upon the bottom of the boats to keep the ice from forming on it.

A few days later, I got a message from General Cadwalader informing me that he had taken his small army of about 1,000 men into New Jersey—where any future action would likely take place. He suggested that I return to New

Jersey. So I took my men back across the Delaware. At our staff meeting there, we decided to set up a defensive perimeter at Trenton—well aware that the British would be hotly pursuing us. Our entire strategy depended, however, on enough of my men re-enlisting for us to even have an Army.

I treated these farmers, merchants and craftsmen as men of honor, who were entitled to equality of esteem. My officers followed my example, addressing even the privates as "gentlemen." No other army at that time did so, or—for that matter—any other society. I helped to introduce the concept that the term "gentleman" referred to a moral quality rather than a social rank. It was a new American idea of honor, which was not defined by birth, rank, status, or wealth, but by the principle of human dignity and respect. Men treated like this would be loyal to our cause.

We assembled the re-enlisted Army along with others from various detachments who had since joined us at Trenton on January 2, 1777. We awaited the onslaught of the British Army. I had fewer than 6,000 colonials. The British had nearly 9,000 of the best professional troops in the world, with their best general, Cornwallis, leading them.

I had dispatched a portion of our Army earlier to the road from Princeton to Trenton to harass the progress of the British. They succeeded very well, causing the British to take eight hours to cover what usually took four. Normally to divide forces in the face of an enemy is risky, but here I had calculated correctly.

Upon the British Army's arrival in Trenton it was nearly dusk; Cornwallis held his council of war. As usual with the British, only the senior officer decides on a course of action. Cornwallis thought he had us trapped, so (after a few desultory probes) he decided to delay his attack until morning. A few of his top officers objected, but had to obey his wishes.

I too held a council, but I let everyone speak freely. A young officer told me of a back road that led to Princeton. Using this road, I circled back around Cornwallis and attacked the weakened garrison left behind at Princeton, with the result of another resounding victory!

I might have attempted then to lead my men on to Brunswick to capture the British treasure war chest, which might have ended the war. However, my men were too exhausted to go further. They had been marching and fighting with no sleep for 36 hours. What we had won was reward enough. In my written report to Congress, and thus to the American people, I gave all credit for success to the men.

Procter and Gamble (P&G) was in difficulty a number of years ago when a new CEO by the name of Alan (A. G.) Lafley took over. He did not stay seated behind his desk, but immediately started visiting employees out in the field. He sought to establish a personal relationship with his employees. He wanted to prove to them that he cared about their welfare by understanding their hopes and aspirations. In addition, Lafley wanted his employees to know the principles for which he stood.

In a visit to a field office, he walked over to an employee working at a desk, stuck out his hand, and asked him about his work. After listening respectfully, Lafley looked the man in the eye and said, “The work you’re doing is vital to the success of Procter and Gamble.”

A longtime P&G employee himself, Lafley showed an appreciation for meaningful work. He rewarded the employee immediately by praising his efforts and acknowledging his value to the company. By building these kinds of relationships with his colleagues at every level, Lafley was able to effect a turnaround at P&G, which resulted in a doubling of price per share of P&G stock in a relatively short time.

To influence your work force to become superior performers you should set an example for them:

- Show pride in your own good work habits.
- Continually learn by observing and listening to others.

- Help them plan their work ahead by formulating a plan together.
- Conduct counseling meetings that contribute to higher degrees of loyalty.

Effective leaders bring people together to achieve sustainable results over a long time. Effective leaders empower people. As people fulfill their responsibility you must reward them appropriately and promptly. You must passionately pursue your retention goals by making integrity a corporate culture, establishing solid relationships, and demonstrating self-discipline. Employees today demand personal relationships before giving themselves fully to their jobs and staying there.

The old style of leadership was by command and control. The new style of collective leadership stresses that employees must be engaged and energized. This is especially necessary with the coming shortage of workers caused by America's declining birth rates. In a tight labor market, negligent companies are likely to lose people to more progressive companies. With a severe lack of qualified people, there will be fierce competition for good producers.

In the eyes of the people who report directly to you, you are the most meaningful part of the company. To earn and keep their trust, you must hold on to your values—and this means no lying, cheating, stealing, or taking false credit. In other words you must always act ethically.

The 20th-century notion of success was in grabbing money, power, and prestige. Things are different today. Many now redefine their success as to what they can do for others. Effective leaders often sacrifice their own feelings to achieve a success that will benefit others. They recognize that their contributions can change the face of earth.

Many of the very wealthy of today—like Bill Gates and Warren Buffett—are giving huge sums to charity. Buffett is also the epitome of ethical leadership. He sits on and guides 20 boards of directors. He makes money and promotes other people's careers, always by operating within ethical lines. He gives his employees the opportunity to do their jobs the way they think best. He doesn't hover over them or distrust them. He keeps his hands off direct operational control of the over 100 companies in his portfolio. He is, however, always ready to help.

The CEO of one of Buffett's companies, Chuck Higgins of Sees Candy, says this of Buffett: "I don't feel I'm his employee or a provider of things he wants the company to do, but that I am his friend and confidant. Right from the beginning and ever since, he has treated me as a partner and an equal. He wants people to work as though the company was the sole asset for his family. To act like the owner. His people think that they have more than a contract with Buffett but have a covenant."

Buffett's company, Berkshire-Hathaway, is one of the most successful companies in history. People like to feel part of and proud of a successful team. Good performers don't leave successful teams.

Herb Kelleher of Southwest Airlines did not micromanage his people either. He knew that overly close supervision is bad for the long-term growth of a company. That kind of management (as opposed to leadership) diminishes the confidence of workers, saps their initiative, and stifles their ability to think for themselves when called upon to solve problems. Micro-managing is counter-productive to the best interests of both company and individual.

When it came to rewarding productivity, Kelleher gave his people as much in the package of total benefits as possible. Southwest Airlines fairly shared its earnings with its employees, which kept resentment at bay. Kelleher made sure everyone shared in the profits and—most importantly—let his employees know that the company's success was a direct result of their efforts.

One company published its the ultimate rule book for its employees:

Rule #1: Use your best judgment at all times.
Rule #2: Refer to Rule #1.

Your good performers remain loyal with this type of discretionary freedom.

Anger, fear, apathy, and sullen silence among the work force are signs of a dissonant company. In a survey of 1,000 companies 43% of the respondents said they witnessed yelling and verbal abuse in the workplace. These are classic signs of dissonance. Arrogant bosses who attack the character of employees inflict toxic emotional abuse. Character attacks are extremely stressful to the recipient. Stress causes a fight or flight syndrome. If a worker feels too weak to fight his superior, then his only recourse is flight. In either case, he usually takes this toxic stress home, thus upsetting his family relationships as well.

Employees hate bosses who de-motivate, create apathy and cause resentment. They tend to do as little as possible. They just want to get by and stay out of trouble. This is the death knell for productivity.

Starbucks, led by founder Howard Schultz, took a giant step to establish a positive attitude of loyalty within its work force, even before it began making a profit. It provided comprehensive health care for everyone. It has been proven that companies that take social responsibility for the welfare of their employees fare better on the bottom line. After it started making money, Starbucks gave everyone ownership in the company via stock options. This encouraged everyone to think and act like owners of the company.

The Harvard Center for Public Leadership teaches executives to understand and control their emotions. The executives are encouraged to develop an appreciation of how their behavior influences others. A calm demeanor promotes maximum effectiveness. Author Daniel Goleman calls this "emotional intelligence." Yelling, screaming and throwing temper tantrums are signs of emotional immaturity. This behavior often turns loyal employees disloyal.

John Mackey, a "collective leadership" CEO, co-founded Whole Foods Markets (WFM) in 1978 with $45,000 in capital. His business had $250,000 in sales that first year. In 2006 WFM had $5.6 billion in sales and $200 million in net profits. Mackey led WFM to a market capitalization of over $8 billion.

He made excellent use of a concept he called "Conscious Capitalism." This concept calls for seeking the highest level of profit through indirect actions.

This concept has four major characteristics that he envisioned:

1) "Great Purpose"—to provide the best food and best service for customers while acting in the best interests of everyone, the employees (called team members), the vendors and suppliers, the community, the environment, and the owners (the shareholders) of the company.

2) The "True"—is the excitement of discovering and implementing a new and improved process of service, which features a broader approach—taking into consideration many factors, not just profits—that delivers long term success to all.

3) The "Beautiful"—in which the company provides a pleasing atmosphere where employees search for excellence and stretch for perfection. Employees are encouraged to always seek continuous improvement and are rewarded by more than just money. They gain emotional fulfillment by doing good for others.

4) The "Heroic"—defines the quest to make the world a better place in which to live. The goal is to solve the problem of people eating unhealthy foods, to raise the level of general health, and to encourage good food habits by example and by education.

Mackey set out to achieve what others said was

impossible and has in large part fulfilled his vision. Mackey lets team members run the various departments by empowering them with both authority and responsibility. At WFM, employees don't work just for money. They work for respect by all stake-holders, for a chance to grow, to learn, to do interesting and meaningful work, to be appreciated for their accomplishments, to make a contribution to others and to feel they have a worthwhile purpose in life.

For overall level of excellent service, Whole Foods was voted by *Fortune* magazine as one of top 100 companies in America to work for over the period 1998-2007. In 2007, it was voted number five in that ranking.

Employees will feel little loyalty to stay with companies that perform poorly. They fear for their job security and the worst-case scenario, bankruptcy. At best, the company may not make enough to pay salaries as well as pensions, health care and other benefits. These companies have a crying need to be more productive.

Companies also put the careers of employees at risk by outsourcing, downsizing and hiring part-time and temporary workers. Companies and countries as well suffer from a lack of specialized skills because people will not train or educate themselves if they fear that no job will be available for them.

American corporations have turned over to employees the risk for retirement, health care, and job security. Many companies now dodge paying benefits by hiring only part-time or temporary workers, and by so doing they diminish loyalty. Leaders of companies are not being loyal to their employees if they callously disregard their best interests.

George Washington speaks:

After we had won our independence the states, not in immediate danger from a common enemy, started quarreling and bickering among themselves. I feared our tenuous union would fall apart and we'd be taken over by a foreign power. I pressed for a constitutional convention. As its president, I helped write the American constitution. To become effective, however, it must be ratified by the states.

In many states, the vote for ratification of the Constitution had been very close. In Virginia—my home state—it only passed by a vote of 89 to 79. If Virginia had not ratified the Constitution, I could not have been president for I would not have been a citizen of the new United States.

To show the people the majesty of the new government and gain their loyalty to our new nation, I decided to travel northeast and south early in my first administration. I would meet with all the local leaders personally and instill in them an appreciation of the new federal government. The final trip (and by far the longest) was to the south. I left Philadelphia in April 1791 and returned in June. I went down to Savannah by the seacoast route, and then returned inland through Augusta, Georgia and Charlotte, North Carolina. My goal was eight hours a day at five miles an hour.

During the trip, I stayed only in public accommodations and never accepted private charity. There were two reasons for this. First, I wanted the people to feel free to visit me without fear of trespassing on private property. Second, I did not want to be beholden to those with whom I stayed. In addition, if I had accepted hospitality from one, the rest might feel resentful that I had not stayed with them.

I viewed it to be a necessity to instill among the people an appreciation of our new government in order to retain their loyalty.

Retaining Superior Performers
George Washington speaks:

In one of the most critical speeches of my military career, I convinced my Army officers to remain loyal to our glorious cause. I spoke to them on March 15, 1783 as the war was winding down, but before a final peace treaty had been signed. Many officers wanted to march on Congress and establish a military dictatorship. They felt that Congress had treated them unfairly. That they had been treated unfairly was true, but it was not entirely the fault of Congress. Congress had no power of enforcement over the States. The country was woefully short on resources and the states were not fulfilling their commitments to the Army.

With no access to funds, Congress had not paid many of the officers for several years. Now that the war appeared to be nearly won, many officers thought that Congress was reneging on promised future pensions. They wanted to take government power into their own hands before the Congress disbanded the Army.

I could have chosen to lead them and establish myself as dictator. Instead, I appealed to them to remember that we had previously shared everything together. If they mutinied now and seized political power, they would be giving up forever the prize of establishing a country of political freedoms. The officers agree to stay loyal, which set a precedent that the Army has honored ever since. America is one of the few countries in the world to have never been ruled by a military dictatorship.

Superior performers contribute most to a company's productivity. Companies must make every effort keep their good people and not lose them to competitors. They are too hard and too costly to replace. Studies show that 70% of American companies report a shortage of qualified leaders, even though companies spend fortunes each year on training and educating their employees. If employees feel that they are valued and appreciated, they tend to be more loyal and are more likely to stay.

The Whole Foods Market vision, as developed by founder John Mackey, was to serve the best food at the fairest price. Mackey endowed the company with a strong sense of purpose. One serves the customers best by satisfying the needs of the people providing the service. Certainly, the owners must maintain legal control, but they are wise to let their employees have freedom in running the company. For examplc, this company lets employees have control of various departments to run as if were their own companies. Every three years, employees get to vote their own mix of fringe benefits.

Whole Foods is known for its equitable sharing of income. Formerly, their top managers got 14 times the wages of the average worker. It now stands at 19 times the wages of the average worker, in order to remain competitive in pay scales to keep their superior performers on board. By contrast, in most large American corporations, the compensation of the average CEO is 431 times that of the average worker.

If the CEO is outstandingly successful in leading his company to high profits by excellent service to the customers, then his compensation may be justified. Often, however, the CEO fails in his duties but gets grossly overpaid anyway. This is not only unfair, but sends a negative message to all stakeholders in the company as well as to the public at large. Employees, who are aware of this abuse, have low morale and are less loyal. In the best-led companies, every effort is made to have employees, including the CEOs, paid according to the value they provide to the company.

In 2007, Whole Foods' CEO, John Mackey, decided against taking a salary in order to set an example. To establish a sense of fairness among its employees, WFM allocates 93% stock options to them with only 7% going to the top executives—a total of 16 people. In the average Fortune 500 American corporation, the top five executives get 75% of the pie, while all the rest of employees get 25%. The WFM system is much more equitable. In 2006, John Mackey was voted by *Barron's* to be among the world's top 30 CEOs for leadership and industry stature.

The employees of a company are its most valuable asset. The best way for a CEO to influence his company's future is to create it. The more productive his key performers are, the better the future that can be created. The first thing Washington did upon taking charge of the Army in July 1775 was to convince the men of the value of working together to achieve their jointly shared vision. The necessity of retaining your best people is often overlooked. It is, however, one of the most critical qualities of leadership. Your superior performers contribute most to the productivity necessary to achieve the goals of your company.

George Washington on his Horse

The Cost of Losing Your Best

To be most productive and profitable, companies must

keep their good workers. It is very expensive to have to replacc one. Human resource departments report that it can easily cost as much as three years' annual salary to get and train a qualified replacement.

One cost often overlooked is the lost production during the transition period. More easily recognizable are costs for exit interviews, hiring, training, and getting everyone accustomed to a new environment. With a new person on board, even old- timers are thrust into a new environment.

Washington begged Congress for the entire war to give him men with long-term enlistments. He felt that a permanent standing army is not as prone to dislocations of its established processes with the entry of new people.

Most companies offer material fringe benefit rewards to retain the people they want to keep. In addition to increasing the financial package, companies would be well advised to ensure that the employee feels that he is doing meaningful work. Loyalty stems from acknowledgement of real contribution to the company and out to the larger community.

Today, opportunities for self-improvement loom large in the decision of every employee's decision to stay or leave. The findings of a March 2007 survey indicate that companies should treat their employees as though they were customers. This includes providing the type of environment to make them love working for the company.

Retention starts with recruiting. The better the organization matches the person with the position, the higher the retention rate. People and jobs should be compatible. A round worker in a square hole will neither be truly productive nor stress free.

Treat the root cause and not the symptom. If an employee gets a headache doing his job, he shouldn't take Prozac or any other stress-relieving medication. He should find a job he enjoys doing. If a match can't be made within the company, it is better to have the employee go to an environment where his efforts won't frustrate him. He will experience no more stress headaches. His pride and happiness in his new position will undoubtedly lead to a higher level of productivity.

To retain good employees, a company must have an ethics culture. No quality employee wants to work for a crook. They realize that—if their employer cheats others—he will cheat them as well. Within ethical companies—those who have a culture to do the best for all their stakeholders—employees know that they will be listened to, appreciated, and respected by their leaders.

Employees also want the freedom to learn. They want an opportunity to be creative in change and even to fail without being unduly punished. Companies must provide employees with a challenge to achieve higher productivity. The top three features that companies must provide to retain good people are (1) an opportunity for personal growth; (2) support from the top; and (3) a comprehensive learning atmosphere.

Sam Walton, founder of Wal-Mart, had this good advice on retention: "Outstanding leaders go out of their way to boost the self-esteem of their personnel. If people believe in themselves, it's amazing what they can accomplish."

A Gallup poll conducted during the 20-year period from 1986 to 2006, with over a million employees and 80,000 managers interviewed, had some interesting findings. In determining what would affect the level of employee morale and retention rates, a high number of respondents rated their immediate managers as the most important factor within the company. In other words, the respondents tend to judge the entire company by the person to whom they directly report. The implication is clear. It behooves companies to focus at *all* levels of leadership education to help upgrade the skills necessary to successfully increase retention rates.

Your most valuable employees are the ones who take best advantage of the opportunities offered by the company. Don Burris of Burris Research wrote, "It's not the tools you have but how you use them. Keeping your key performers is the key factor for the long term success and profitability of your business."

To be the most effective you should start the retention process even before the new employee's first day. Write your new hire beforehand to tell her what you expect of her and what you will provide in return. Have her future team members write her a welcome letter. In it, they should offer to help her get properly adjusted. Be there yourself on the first day to welcome her. Assign each team member a particular duty to welcome the new hire. Give her a roster of fellow team members names and their duties so she can get to know right away how best to fit in.

Do all you can to make life easy for your people by offering collateral low-cost fringe benefits, such as laundry service, baby-sitting, day care, health club, flex time, and carpooling. They will appreciate your thoughtfulness in making their lives simpler.

To encourage the highest morale among your people, you must first be an opportunity leader and not a crisis manager. Opportunities are positive, crises are negative. Opportunities are pro-active and crises are reactive. Opportunities lead to unlimited profit potential through productivity growth. Solved crises save only the resources at risk. Effective leaders don't spend all their time putting fires out.

John Quincy Adams, our sixth President, said it well: "If your actions inspire others to dream more, learn more, do more, and become more, you are a leader."

A 2000 Gallup poll indicated that 71% of American workers are not actively engaged in their work. Their inattention costs employers almost $350 billion a year. Only actively engaged workers are the key performers that you want to retain.

Trust in the ethical policies of their companies influences people to stay. What type of CEO behavior earns trust? It is those CEOs who respond constructively to their employees' problems, who thoughtfully consider their ideas, who recognize their achievements, who are honest and truthful, who help them grow and develop and who give them clear and logical directions.

George Washington speaks:

After our victory at the Battle of Trenton, I lined my men up by regiments. Astride my great horse Nelson, I faced the men and asked them to re-enlist with these words: "My brave fellows, You have done all I have asked you to do, and more than could be reasonably expected, but your country is at stake, your wives, your houses and all that you hold dear."

"You have worn yourselves out with fatigue and hardships, but we know not how to spare you. If you will consent to stay only one month longer, you will render that service to the cause of liberty, and to your country, which you probably never can do under any such circumstances. This is the crisis which is to decide our destiny."

I backed off to the side of the assembled men to await their answer. None stepped forward. Again I went before the men and spoke to them, overcome with emotion.

A sergeant later described the scene: "The General personally addressed us … told us our services were greatly needed, and that we could do more now for our country than we could most likely ever do again, and in the most affectionate manner entreated us to stay."

Recognizing that patriotism alone wasn't enough, I offered each man a $10 bonus. At that time I didn't think I had authority to offer them government money, but I was willing to mortgage or sell Mount Vernon for the money. I wasn't yet aware that Congress had shortly before given me authority to commit government funds!

After a number of men had stepped forward to re-enlist, the officer in charge asked me, "Sir, should I enroll these men?"

"No," I replied, "Men who will volunteer in such a case as this need no signed enrollment papers to keep them to their duty."

The men who re-enlisted knew what they getting into. A veteran later recalled that one/half of those men who re-enlisted that day were dead within the year.

Success breeds success. New enlistments and re-enlistments soared as American volunteers flocked to us. They were given a small bounty of cash and the promise of 100 acres of free land when the war was won. Men want to serve with organizations they respect as winners.

British Captain John Bowater—referring to the 10 days of victories and actions that changed the future of world government wrote, "By these and other artful methods, they prevailed upon their people to re-enlist, and now they have got a very considerable army together."

In all my endeavors, I understood the value of keeping and promoting the men who were most committed to our jointly shared vision and mission. I wrote to James McHenry, "It is infinitely better to have a few good men than many indifferent ones."

American businesses spend an estimated $4-7 billion annually recruiting employees who they think will make a real contribution to their company. Some will indeed be good performers. The more of these people they can retain, the better for the customers, the company's other employees, management, and shareholders. The value of a retained employee includes all you have invested in them—knowledge, training, education and experience—plus the value of your intellectual property that they know. Departed employees take all this with them.

Another big cost to American businesses are employees who may be physically present but disengaged emotionally and mentally from their work. The same principles used to retain employees are also those that will re-engage and re-energize your work force. Make the best use of precious resources by helping your managers become more skilled as retention leaders.

The Harvard Center for Public Leadership reports that 56% of Americans they polled were not proud of their immediate supervisors, 66% of those polled said that we are in a leadership crisis, and 75% felt that America would decline unless we improved our leadership. 83% of workers polled said that their corporate executives were more concerned with short-term bottom line results than by running the company well. No wonder so many employees become disillusioned and leave.

The following concepts are credited to David Ewing, executive editor of Harvard Business Review. He also authored the book, "Freedom within the Corporation." High retention of good performers strengthens companies. To retain good performers companies should adhere to what might be called an "Employee Bill of Rights." This covenant honors these principles of providing their work force an environment where employees will:

1. Feel that they are a part of cause worthy of their commitment.
2. Be mentally challenged in a meaningful job.
3. Be trusted by management – not hovered over and micro-managed.
4. Given great latitude to work independently.
5. Be treated honestly, fairly and with respect.
6. Be given every opportunity for self-improvement.
7. Be part of a supportive and caring work environment.
8. Feel truly involved in the mission.
9. Be given free rein to voice their opinions without fear of retribution.
10. Be allowed to provide uninhibited feedback.
11. Be free to make mistakes, for that is how one learns.

The Harvard Center for Public Leadership cites these proven concepts to retain good people:

- Provide an opportunity for everyone to build a shared sense of responsibility with the company.
- Make all feel that they are making a positive social impact.
- Implement an innovative strategy to achieve sustainable results both in breath and depth of service to all stakeholders.
- Encouragement to exceed their wildest dreams.

Employees leave their companies because they feel:

1. unappreciated
2. that their work is not meaningful
3. that they are treated unfairly
4. that they are not recognized for accomplishments
5. that they are not being listened too
6. that they are left out of the decision-making loop
7. that their manager thinks of them more as a problem than the solution to increased productivity
8. that they are assigned a boring job without possibility for self-improvement

Effective retention leaders avoid making the above mistakes.

According to Jennifer Hodges, Director of Compensation and Benefits for AARP, "Corporate productivity is directly related to the retention of capable, loyal, and ethical employees who are placed in jobs where they can make the most contribution now and developed for critical roles in the future."

David M. Alexander was the Manager of Distribution

(Retired) for a Fortune 500 industrial gas company. He is an excellent example of the value of continually learning. Back in the mid-80's doing fairly well with APD in the Houston regional office, he decided to get a MBA while still working full time. With his MBA in hand he embarked upon a meteoric rise in responsibilities within his company. He was very generous to provide the insights that he learned:

"There are two major factors that have a significant impact on profitability in a positive way in today's workplace environment. They are technology and productivity."

"Technology provides opportunities for step change improvements in efficiencies, productivity and profits. However, technology normally requires significant capital investment and may take considerable time to develop and implement."

"Productivity improvements, especially those identified and implemented by the employee(s), can produce significant changes and at a cost far less than technological changes and generally can be implemented in a shorter period of time. The keys to employee driven productivity programs are willingness by management and employees to make changes and improvements in current practices and processes and a sense on the employee's part that management is willing to listen to ideas from the workforce."

"The greater the effort on management's part to communicate to employees about all aspects of the business and to foster a feeling of empowerment on the part of the work force, the greater the understanding of the needs and goals of the organization by employees. This leads to greater buy-in by employees on the objectives of the organization and also educates employees as to the needs of the business. Willingness of management to listen to ideas from the individuals and groups that are performing tasks fosters increased input of improvement ideas. These concepts can also contribute to increased employee morale. As more and more legitimate and worthwhile ideas are recognized and implemented by management, the more 'ownership' empowerment and support are generated by the workforce."

"Recognition of employee input and ideas, both public and private, continues to feed employee self-esteem and morale continues to improve, productivity increases and profits are boosted. In addition, as morale improves, turnover of employees is reduced. Improved employee retention lowers the cost to the organization by increasing attendance on the job, reducing hiring and training costs and minimizes the lost productivity involved in getting new employees up to the level of proficiency of a former employee. A loyal and stable workforce will enhance productivity by virtue of the knowledge and experience that the employees possess."

"Throughout my career, those operating organizations with the highest morale and the most open-minded leadership produced the highest productivity and were the most profitable in our organization."

Marilyn Nelson, CEO of Carlson Companies (one of 11 women CEOs of Fortune 500 companies), is an expert on retention. She says, "A company must invest in educating all leader managers on the best techniques to retain top performers."

There must be a positive relationship between leader and worker. There must be trust between the two, as it should be in all our relationships.

Retention starts with a positive attitude at the top. If a company's environment is negative, its employees are often suspicious, backbiting, and sabotaging. This hurts productivity. Effective leaders use feedback to overcome negativity by asking what is needed to turn around negative feelings. They keep employees informed by keeping them in the loop.

On the other hand a resonant company enjoys a high level of retention. Within resonant companies, employees exhibit tremendous creative power. Their active involvement results in a meaningful development process. The company makes the best use of talent by getting the most out of people.

Workers are loyal and tend to stay.

Successful entrepreneur Richard Branson, founder of the Virgin Companies, says that acting immorally is bad for business. Aligning your grand vision with your ethical values promotes retention and therefore productivity.

Exit interviews are critical. The National Business Research Institute (NBRI) counsels that companies can learn why they are experiencing high turnover by skillful use of exit interviews. It's much more than just saying goodbye and wishing well. It's a chance to dig deep to find out what can be corrected. One of the NBRI clients reduced turnover by 80% using proven exit interview techniques. The company applied what they learned to make course corrections for this successful outcome.

Every CEO should have all his company leaders and managers develop these eleven retention competencies:

1. Earn trust by always acting with integrity.
2. Build your employees esteem.
3. Always exhibit optimism.
4. Don't treat everyone the same.
5. Do not waste the vitally important first ninety days of employment.
6. Help employees develop their inner person.
7. Help the company become one that everyone wants to work for.
8. Reward and praise appropriately.
9. Learn from exit interviews.
10. Assess subtle signs of dissatisfaction as early as possible.
11. Learn how to overcome dissatisfaction.

Here are some additional keys that effective leaders use to unlock the door to better retention.

- Always demonstrate ethical values.

- Have a short fuse for dishonesty, insincerity and lying.
- Have a long fuse for innovation, creativity, experimentation and uniqueness.
- Know that mistakes will happen so be ready to give constructive critiques.
- Groom your replacement so you can move up.
- Say what you mean and mean what you say.
- Make your employees work exciting, stimulating, challenging, fascinating and fun.

One of America's leading management authorities, Warren Bennis, lists the following traits as necessary within company leadership for maximum retention: vision, trust, participation, learning, diversity, creativity, integrity, communication and ethics.

Why are efforts within many companies to improve retention failing so miserably? This is true despite money, time and effort devoted to it. One major factor is a poor relationship with immediate bosses. It is important that leaders at every level are sensitive to Abraham Maslow's hierarchy of human needs:

1. physical and biological.
2. security and safety.
3. sense of belonging to a worthwhile community.
4. a strong feeling of self esteem.
5. a sense of self-development.
6. self-actualization which is growth in dealing with others and environment.

According to management consultant, Warren Bennis, there are certain aspects of corporate culture that can enhance the retention of good workers:

- Inclusion

- Collaboration
- Celebration of diversity
- Process awareness
- Honest communication
- Risk taking
- Individual and team growth

Steps taken to retain your best workers will pay off in performance, productivity, and profitability.

George Washington Resigning His Commission

Chapter Five – Planning For Succession

To ensure that American businesses are headed by effective leaders, we must develop enough qualified leaders to meet the future demand. Polls show there will be a shortage of qualified leaders in the future. To insure having a sufficiency in the future, companies must have a formal policy of developing their own leaders.

Therefore, succession planning is key to long-range success of any organization. It protects against impending crises. Retirement, resignation, poor performance, and death can result in a loss of key talent. We must have leaders with integrity, vision, and competency. A company's very existence is at great risk if they do not build a pipeline full of future talent.

Most companies agree that succession planning is a necessary corporate strategy. Many are slow, however, to commit resources of time, people and money to implement it.

A lack of succession programs—or one poorly executed or even one tolerating substandard efforts—seriously undermines an organization's efforts. A good plan ensures continued superior productivity by building successor leaders at all levels within the company.

Since no one lives nor works forever, succession planning is a vital necessity. Succession planning strategies can be internal or external. Promoting from within is often the most effective. It opens up opportunity positions in order that all employees within the company can be lifted up, just as a rising tide raises all ships.

Senior executives must think widely and deeply about the future of their companies. The goal is not just to replace like with like, but to look at every vacancy as an opportunity to place someone better than the one replaced. They must carefully analyze what types of talent and skill will be most likely needed in the company's future. It could be risky in the sense of spending resources now to prepare for what may happen far down the road. The alternative of not being prepared with a succession plan, however, jeopardizes the very life of the company.

To be fully prepared for future contingencies, the CEO and the top echelon should not only identify good prospects early but also start training them. Making them stretch now and testing their forward thinking will determine if they have the skills and talents needed. Each CEO must create his own diagnostic tools to assess what is needed. The CEO must be involved personally and be an integral part of the process. In fact, all management must participate to make succession planning truly effective. Some companies value succession planning so highly that they make it a part of executive compensation—the better they are in developing new leaders, the higher their compensation.

Succession planning is necessary at all levels within a company. Isolating the process at the very top levels is not enough. A good start is to make fast-track employees visible within the company as early as possible in their tenure. This can be accomplished by learning of and recognizing their current knowledge and interim achievements, thus, making them more widely accepted by the others as they move up the ladder. Internal succession opens an avenue for all to advance. Each qualified person is promoted to the next highest level, which brings with it a new perspective. This brings in fresh air. Old-timers in new positions can make a positive change as well.

Andrew Carnegie said of J. P. Morgan, "He hires his men from outside, I grow mine."

Here are some examples of companies who adopted successful strategies for growing their own successors.

In 1997, Andy Grove, founder and CEO of Intel, became ill with cancer. He was already overburdened with the stress resulting from changes in technology and market conditions. Grove realized that he was too ill to lead the company alone. He needed first-rate help. In May 1998 Grove appointed Craig Barrett his co-leader, with the idea that he would later become his successor. As Intel COO, Barrett had done a good job with operations and manufacturing processes.

Grove realized that Intel must always have excellent people in order to overcome the serious continuing challenges it faced. As CEO, it was Grove's responsibility to lead in evaluating future needs and develop those employees with the ability to fulfill those needs. Grove built a pipeline of talent. His preparations led to reduced employee stress, as the company moved personnel along at the proper speed, and had them ready to assume responsibility whenever needed.

Sam Walton, founder of Wal-Mart, appointed David Glass as his successor in 1992. Walton needed someone extraordinarily well-qualified to continue the sales gains, cost reductions, empowerment, production and all the factors that had made Wal-Mart so profitable. Walton—ever perceptive of business needs—had been planning for his successor well in advance.

Upon his appointment, Glass told the public that Wal-Mart would continue to find better ways of doing things and would be relentless in its search for excellence. His remarks are reminiscent of Hannibal. When that general was asked how he was going to get his elephants over the Alps, he replied, "I'll find a way or I'll make one."

Before Walton's death in 1992, he made audacious plans for 2000. Glass made them all come true. The CEO must play the key role in succession planning, for his choice will continue or break the legacy he has established.

Coca-Cola grows its successors through internal processes. The untimely death of Coke's CEO, Robert Goizueta, proved that no organization can rely on one leader no matter how good he may be. The life expectancy for American CEOs has been getting shorter. Coke's business kept on growing smoothly after Goizueta's death because he had groomed an excellent successor, Doug Ivester. Before his death, Goizueta called Ivester "my partner." Many major divisions within Coke were already reporting to Ivester even before Goizueta became very ill.

Warren Buffett said that Mr. Goizueta's greatest legacy was the way in which he carefully selected and then nurtured the future leadership of the company.

Goizueta had also fostered 12 key people under Ivester—each of whom had talented protégés of his own. A company cannot have too much depth of leadership in reserve. Ivester has since created an informal co-leadership at Coke. *Fortune* magazine writer, Betsy Morris, described Ivester's leadership techniques: "Formal hierarchy is out; everyone has knowledge they carry with them. The CEO elevated on a pedestal is out; the CEO as the platoon leader is in."

The Jack Welch story at General Electric (GE) is fascinating and illustrative of superior succession planning. Reginald Jones, CEO of General Electric, had appointed Jack Welch as his successor. He thought Welch could best lead in implementing some much-needed change within the company.

Appointing Welch turned out to be an excellent move for GE's future.

Successful succession planning needs a total commitment from all within the company—particularly in the executive suite. Welch, focused and passionate, provided that dedication. To fulfill future leadership requirements, he needed a pool of highly qualified potential candidates. To create this reserve, Welch stressed rotation and education training within GE. He probed deep within the company to find those he felt could master the necessary core competencies. Once found, he initiated development processes. Welch spoke later of his task as CEO:

"My main job was developing talent. I was a gardener providing water and other nourishment to our top 750 people. Of course, I had to pull out some weeds."

In 1981 GE had 350 divisions with a huge diversity. The company was worth $12 billion and was the world's 11th largest corporation. Welch determined that each division must be first or second in the world in terms of profitability. He developed leadership to run each division. He personally approved over 500 sub managers and leaders. He sold, closed or divested many divisions that did not meet his criteria. GE ended up with 14 world-class businesses. By 1989 it was the world's most valuable company.

In his early days, Welch used fear and coercion as a management technique. When questioned about it later, he answered that it was necessary because of circumstances at that time. He got results by surrounding himself with good people. He created America's strongest management team—one that had purpose and vision.

People who immediately grasp what you teach are unusually motivated to learn. They are good candidates for promotion. Only leaders can build leaders. You can't give to others what you don't possess yourself. For proof of Welch's system, look at the long list of CEOs of other companies who are former executives at GE.

Companies must be willing to spend dollars on developing high potential leaders. Under Jack Welch, GE spent $500 million developing their own internal leadership institute.

Effective leaders do what brings the greatest reward. Mere action is no substitute for achievement.

Degussa, one of the world's largest specialty chemicals company, developed a proven competency model based on the company's vision, mission and guidance principles. Their model helps them determine where the company is going, as well as identifying and developing those employees with adequate capabilities to fulfill those critical roles. A succession plan is critical for an organization to continue to flourish. Company approval to develop talent is a necessity, but it risks time and resources. Mark Twain recognized that when he wrote, "The art of prophecy is very difficult, especially with respect to the future."

George Washington speaks:

Valley Forge was the crucible where I forged a new professional army that went on to win our independence at Yorktown. I used every opportunity to build future leaders—a vital necessity in warfare, with sickness and death from wounds taking its daily toll.

Each day the senior officers and I had our main midday meal together, during which we customarily discussed vitally important military matters. I started inviting junior officers, on a rotating basis, to attend. I made it competitive for them so that it was an honor to be invited. This gave the young officers an extra incentive to be better leaders of their own men. During the extended mealtime, I relaxed the normal rules of strict military etiquette to encourage the young men to speak their minds. There was even a moderate amount of passing the bottle around to loosen tongues—but never to the point of drunkenness. Those who did over imbibe were not invited back. I had several objectives in mind:

- *to boost morale and keep it high;*

- *to bring out the best in each man;*
- *to re-enforce our vision and mission;*
- *to evaluate each man's capabilities;*
- *to learn who was accomplishing their goals; and*
- *to rank the men who were most qualified for promotion.*

I took men as they were—not as I wished them to be. I felt that we could make each man better, so I did everything possible to bring out the best from each man.

I made it a priority to "honor the messenger"—as those younger officers brought valuable information. They were encouraged to relate the problems they faced and how they solved them; what opportunities they foresaw and how they planned to take advantage of them. The younger officers—proud to be asked their opinion—felt a part of the decision-making process. It encouraged them to think.

Being careful to never monopolize nor dominate the discussions, I was rather taciturn as I listened attentively and made a point of showing respect for each contributor. I needed to know the bad along with the good. I was affable, but always kept a proper reserve so that all the officers, while feeling comfortable in my presence, would never forget that I was the commander-in-chief. I was teaching them another skill—that of communication—on how to become our civilian leaders of the future, a vital part of our succession planning.

We senior officers used this opportunity to instill even deeper within the junior ones the vision for which we were contending. Yes, we would say, today things are bleak, but just over the horizon is a time when we will be free of British tyranny. We will all live in a land of milk and honey with our wives and children, enjoying liberty and justice for all. In the relaxed conversational atmosphere, the senior officers were able to make a more accurate evaluation of the capabilities of the younger officers and the depth of their commitment to the cause. Consequently, when time came for assignments and promotions, the senior officers were able to make far better choices than merely looking at a list of names on a sheet of paper.

As my men were amateur soldiers—having been farmers and tradesmen before volunteering to serve—they were ignorant of military skills. These sessions were a learning experience in the art of war. The older, more experienced officers instructed the younger.

Soldiers must be supplied, so we sent out foraging parties to gather food and supplies. The British also sent out foragers. I ordered special units out to harass the British foragers. Our parties of men ranged from several dozen to several hundred, led mostly by junior officers. The performance of the officers in these relatively minor, but important, positions was evaluated in the midday mess meetings. The leaders of the sorties would report to the group their experiences and all attendees were urged to constructively critique. Participants learned from their own experience, as well as from the experience of others.

The midday mess helped create a talented corps of young officers and proved successful in a broader sense. We not only developed military leaders we needed but also a long line of future civilian leaders—the most well-known of whom were Alexander Hamilton, James Monroe and John Marshall. Hamilton formulated the economic plans in my first administration that have enabled us to become the most prosperous nation on earth. Monroe, the fifth President of the United States, is best known for the Monroe Doctrine, which kept European powers from ravaging the American continents. John Marshall, later the renowned Chief Justice of the Supreme Court, was also a young officer under my command.

In March 2005, a nine-year Walt Disney veteran Roger Iger was chosen to replace Michael Eisner as CEO of that company. The Board's choice of an insider showed confidence in Disney's internal talent. Many companies still don't have succession planning processes in place. Why? Because they think they can recruit the necessary talent from outside the company whenever it is needed. That is no longer true. Twenty years ago, according to Jeffrey Sonnenfeld, Associate Dean at Yale's School of Management, seven percent of companies hired outside CEOs. Now that number is 50%. This translates as tremendous competition for talent.

Hiring from outside is also expensive, but not only in monetary terms. It also reduces the chance of a new CEO's being successful. A Booz Allen Hamilton study of 2500 companies showed that home-grown CEOs average about 2% better performance each year over the seven years that they measured. Companies that go outside for its CEO send the negative message to its senior executives that not one of them was considered worthy of promotion.

Stanford researchers, James Collins and Jerry Porras, found that companies such as Procter & Gamble, Wal-Mart, GE and Sony are visionary and have succession plans in effect. Leading companies such as these are six times more likely to promote from within.

In the past, companies without plans were not hurt as much as they are today. Turnover was less volatile because CEOs had longer tenures. Times have changed. By neglecting succession planning the coming shortage of qualified leaders could cripple many American companies. A 2005 study by the Corporate Leadership Council found that 72% of companies worried about filling expected vacancies within the next five to seven years. 76% said they felt less than confident in their ability to fill vacated positions.

Settling for leaders who are less than top-quality is expensive to all of a company's stakeholders. Even with an ever-increasing awareness of the necessity of succession planning, only a few companies are doing it and even fewer are doing it well.

Many companies simply ignore succession planning because of employee sensitivity. Consider the recent history of

ABC News. The company knew that Peter Jennings had cancer, but they didn't want to hurt his feelings so they ignored the process of finding a successor. If they had had a plan in place, Jennings could have helped in the selection process and helped his successor fit in. Some companies fear that naming a successor too soon may cause other employees to leave. That fear is overcome with a thorough and fair selection process. The lack of planning often results in poor successor choices, which hurts the company more in the long term.

The best approaches to succession planning seem to be these:

- Tracking the mission critical role process within the company to see where future needs may be;
- Proactively developing a strong internal talent pool to fill these vital roles;
- Developing a pipeline of capable officers who can execute succession plans;
- Alignment of internal talent to fill potential losses; and
- Continually adding and developing new talent to enlarge the pool.

Visionary companies like IBM have used these criteria. They have a reservoir of trained people ready to step in at all levels on a moment's notice. Developing a pipeline of qualified talent rests on these building blocks.

Senior officials must endorse the plans. Jack Welch at GE believed that developing leaders was his top priority, and insisted that all his lower managers follow suit. He personally approved over 500 sub-managers within GE. Partially as a result of Welch's efforts, GE has promoted 85% of its top officers from within.

Promoting from within is good for morale. The one selected as new CEO knows the capabilities of the others.

Some top company presidents schedule defined meetings with prospective candidates throughout the year. Many CEOs, such as Welch, hold managers accountable for development within their own sphere of responsibility. Some even tie manager compensation to it. One company makes up to 30% of total compensation dependent on results of talent development. This ensures that adequate resources of time and money are devoted to it. Talented people are too important to be left hidden within an organization. There should be an ongoing system to bring them to the forefront of attention and recognition.

The CEO must lead to determine which positions are critical for future growth. They must fill a pool of qualified people. The company should develop a competency model to use to constantly re-evaluate executives, in order to identify those who are ready to take over now and those who may be ready to take over later. Everyone within the talent pool should be constantly groomed for larger responsibilities.

Without an ongoing and effective process, the future choices are subjective and based on limited knowledge of a candidate's capabilities. Data may be vague and confusing without guidelines, and could lead to the promotion of those of limited performance ability.

Some companies make the mistake of focusing entirely on the very top echelons. They shortchange themselves if they do not go deeper within the organization, looking for and developing future talent. Every layer should be quality staffed. It is also a mistake to focus just on the "stars" within each category. This approach ignores the unique (though for the moment, latent) talents of others.

Long-term bench strength is essential for effective succession planning. Leadership development is a corporate strategic priority. There should be a range of targeted learning experiences. The company should offer stretch assignments, institute internal and external training, make appointments to executive programs and MBAs, and offer mentoring, coaching, and action learning with special rotation assignments across the entire organization.

Procter & Gamble develops leaders internally by moving them to assignment within regions inside the country and even around the world. They make these assignments last for three to five years, in order that individuals can learn operations and procedures well enough to be most effective in the future. Some companies even appoint executives to serve as volunteers with non-profit organizations to accelerate learning. It is an opportunity to acquire and demonstrate skills beyond their current responsibility, as well as a chance to lead others without having authority over them. Rotary, Kiwanis, Lions and other service clubs have proven to be excellent training grounds for executive talent.

Companies like Home Depot have structured assessment methods of development, which ensure that no talent is overlooked. They never promote without an objective assessment. They give their top 100 people intensive training, which includes a three-week program specifically on leadership, management issues and business challenges. They bring in outside consultants to teach cross-function and cross-business interactions. More companies should follow the Home Depot lead.

Intel has a procedure called "two in a box," in which management functions overlap and executives learn to cover for each other. Here are some of Intel's guidelines:

Never assume that one size fits all. Each division must create its own special plan.

There must be accountability for managing and monitoring. Someone is held responsible.

Techniques and processes cannot stay within the HR department but must go out to line managers.

CEOs must involve line managers at all levels. If excluded, they may be unwilling to devote time, energy and resources to the process. They may also be reluctant to suggest candidates for future promotion, for fear of making a mistake.

Companies must measure their succession planning

victories and failures. Each can be a valuable learning lesson. There should be a two-fold measurement. The first is of the organization itself. The second is of each of the individuals within it. Some companies find the leadership potential of employees difficult to measure, so they don't even attempt it. Other companies have outmoded processes and are out of touch with reality.

All companies should implement model programs that include measurement processes. These ensure an outcome of continuous improvement, such as:

- Filling more leadership jobs internally;
- Creating a higher number of qualified personnel per leadership position;
- Ensuring proper ethnic and gender promotions;
- Increasing the number of positions with two or more "ready now" applicants; and
- Lowering the attrition rate of the talent pool, in order to keep it well stocked.

Organizations must re-evaluate after every promotion. Many do so routinely every three or more years.

Succession plans fail as a result of faulty processes, identified by poor strategy, unclear procedures, lack of cooperation, and frequent changes in methodology. Often there is resistance from managers who do not want to commit resources to the process. Some fear to participate in the election of top talent because of their own insecurities and prejudices.

Eminent philosopher, Walter J. Lippmann, said this about a leader: "The final test of a leader is that he leaves behind him in other men the conviction and will to carry on."

A few years ago, a high-tech company needed a new CEO. Because of their lack of succession planning they had to hire from the outside, which can be risky. They found what they thought was a good prospect from the food industry. They hired him and gave him pretty much *carte blanche*. Naturally, he installed processes that had been proven successful for him before. For example, he set up incentive rewards and recognition promotions based on individual accomplishments, as had been normal in the food business—ignoring his present role as leader of a corporate culture that stresses teamwork over individual efforts.

Rewarding individuals in this type of culture is counter-productive. Teams do the work. His singling out one from among the team for recognition had disastrous consequences for all. Morale sank, people left, and the company sank beneath the waves in a bitter storm of controversy. The company fired the CEO, but it was too late. He had failed them. His earlier success had gotten him into a mindset he couldn't shake loose. CEOs who cannot adapt to changing circumstances put their companies at great risk.

One of the greatest acts of patriotism in American history occurred on 23 December 1783 when General George Washington, Commander of all armed forces in America, appeared before the Continental Congress, then meeting in Annapolis, Maryland. The great man stood tall and erect before them. An unprecedented moment was at hand. A victorious general, the possessor of absolute power, would voluntarily, and with great humility, relinquish his command—a deed seldom, if ever, witnessed in all of history.

Washington addressed the Congressmen formally:

"Having now finished the work assigned me, I retire from the great theatre of action, and bidding an affectionate farewell to this august body under whose orders I have long acted, I here offer my commission, and take my leave of all the employments of public life."

A clear and viable succession plan will ensure a departure with dignity and a legacy of strength and endurance.

George Washington Taking the Oath of Office

Conclusion

Isaac Newton realized the value of learning from those who had gone before when he said, “If I have seen further than others, it is because I was standing on the shoulders of giants.” The leadership principles—as practiced by George Washington—have as much relevance today as they did when our nation was founded. Stand on George Washington’s shoulders.

When corporate cheaters, liars and thieves are exposed to public view, all of American business suffers. The recent media coverage of Enron, WorldCom, Arthur Andersen, Tyco and Global Crossing, to name a few, increases the distrust which Americans have in our capitalistic system. There are lessons here for everyone in business, and the tide is beginning to turn. In the wake of highly-publicized corporate corruption, the issue of corporate ethics is high on the agenda of the business community.

As a result of the Enron and other corporate scandals, Congress enacted the Sarbanes Oxley act in 2002. It mandates that companies exercise strict controls over all financial affairs. Companies must adhere to rigorous reporting measures to the government. If not complied with the government will punish transgressions.

In November 2004 the Federal Sentencing Act went even further by requiring that every company, both private and public, must conduct ethics training classes for all employees. This appears at first glance to be a net cost to the company. By incorporating within these ethics sessions this book on Washington's principles for higher productivity, however, then these classes will also become profit centers. This book should be made a part of every ethics course. It proves that ethical conduct pays big dividends.

The Washington-based Ethics Resource Center (ERC)—celebrating its 85th anniversary throughout 2007—conducts assessment of workplace ethics environments and the promotion of a stronger ethical foundation for society, in America and worldwide. The ERC designed an index of the most ethical companies. They found that their stock market return was 102% over five-year period from 1997 to 2002 versus a 26% return for the S&P 500—four times more favorable. The ERC also tracks companies that have an in-house ethics program, but acknowledges that the modeling behavior of senior executives is still the critical issue.

The International Business Ethics Institute, headquartered in Washington and London, adheres to the concept that the ends do not justify the means, and sponsors programs that promote business ethics as a corporate advantage.

The Institute conducted a survey, which shows that public trust in business leaders is low at 24%—with only politicians and journalists ranked lower. They have succumbed I believe to the temptation President Washington warned against in his letter to Gouverneur Morris. Here is his quote: "I believe it is among nations as it is with individuals, the party taking advantage of the distresses of another will lose infinitely more in the opinion of mankind and in subsequent events than he will gain by the stroke of the moment."

Many professions in America now require periodic continuing education that mandates ethics training. The Society of Financial Service Professionals set up the National Institute of Ethics, to enhance professionalism through ethical standards and integrity training.

To remain "free and happy," we must stamp out the corruption that is destroying the moral fiber of our country. We must withhold our dollars from unethical businesses. We must withhold our votes from crooked politicians. By continuing to honor the principles of ethical conduct ourselves, our example will strengthen the ideals of what it means to be an American. You will prove, just as George Washington did, that nice guys do finish first.

About The Author

Jim Hodges combines his passion for American history with a rock-solid record of performance with some of the nation's largest financial institutions. During his career with John Hancock Insurance Company, Jim was one of the youngest Life Members of the Million Dollar Roundtable—seven consecutive years of over $1 million in annual sales. In sales management, he helped lead his agency to become one of the top ten in the nation.

Hodges' two decades with John Hancock, and his subsequent career with Merrill Lynch, afforded him a fertile field for the study of management processes. He retired as a vice president of Merrill Lynch on January 1, 2005.

Hodges holds a doctorate in Economics, and taught part time for the Business Administration School at the University of Maryland. His study of micro-economics, the theory of the firm, particularly aided him in learning leadership and management principles later out in the real business world. His next book will primarily focus on Washington's management skills. During his business career he earned the professional degrees of Chartered Life Underwriter, Chartered Financial Consultant, Certified Financial Planner and Merrill's Certified Financial Manager. Jim trains executives and staff in principle-centered leadership based on the life of George Washington.

The author resides with his family in Portland, Oregon, where he is an active member of community and civic organizations. Learn more at:

www.leadershipbygeorge.com.

About The Illustrator

Bonnie Hodges is a professional artist in Portland, Oregon. She was born and raised in Washington D.C., has a B.A. in Art from the University of Maryland, and worked as an Illustrator at the U.S. State Department in Washington D.C. She is now a freelance artist with patrons through the United States.

Bonnie's preferred style is Realism. She works with a variety of mediums: oil, pastel, and watercolor, but prefers graphic art. Bonnie's work is on display in collections all around the USA and even Europe. Her work can be viewed online at:

www.cynthiahodges.com/bonnie_art

Bibliography

ABBOTT, W.W. "The Papers of George Washington." Charlottesville: University of Virginia Press, 1994.

ALLEN, W.B. "George Washington, A Collection." Indianapolis: Liberty Classics, 1988.

AMBROSE, STEPHEN and BRINKLEY, DOUGLAS. "Witness to America." New York; Lour Reda Publications, 1999.

AYRES, THOMAS. "That's Not in My American History Book." Dallas: Taylor Trade Publishing, 2000.

BAILEY, THOMAS. "A Diplomatic History of the American People." New York: Meredith Publishing Co., 1964.

BAILEY, THOMAS. "The American Pageant." Boston: D. C. Heath, 1966.

BAILYN, BERNARD. "The Debate on the Constitution." New York: Literary Classics of the United States, 1991.

BENNETT, WILLIAM J. "The Spirit of America." New York: Simon and Schuster, 1997.

BLACK, JEREMY. "War for America." Phoenix: Mill: Wrens Publishing Co. 1998.

BOBRICK, BENSON. "Angel in the 'Whirlwind." New York: Penguin Books, 1997.

BRANDS, H. W. "The First American." New York: Doubleday, 2000.

BROOKHISER, RICHARD. "Alexander Hamilton, American." New York; The Free Press, 1999.

BROOKHISER, RICHARD. "Founding Father." New York: The Free Press, 1996.

CALLOWAY, COLIN. "The American Revolution in Indian Country." Cambridge: Cambridge University Press, 1995.

CARTER, JAMES DAVID. "Masonry in Texas." Waco: Grand Lodge of Texas, 1955.

CHURCH, FORREST. "The American Creed." New York: St. Martin's Press, 2002.

CLARK, HARRISON. "All Cloudless Glory." Washington: Regnery Publishing, Inc., 1995.

COMMAGER HENRY STEELE AND MORRIS, RICHARD B. EDITORS, "The Spirit of Seventy Six, The Story of The American Revolution as Told by Participants." Indianapolis: Bobbs-Merrill, 1958.

CURRENT, RICHARD. "American History." New York; Alfred Knopf, 1959.

DALZELL, ROBERT and DALZELL, LEE. "George Washington's Mount Vernon." New York: Oxford University Press, 1998.

EDITORS OF TIME-LIFE BOOKS. "The Revolutionaries." Alexandria: Time-Life Publications, 1990.

ELLIS, JOSEPH. "Founding Brothers." New York: Alfred Knopf, 2000.

FERLING, JOHN E. "The First of Men." Knoxville: University of Tennessee Press, 1988.

FERLING, JOHN. "Setting the World Ablaze." New York: Oxford University Press, 2000.

FINE, SIDNEY and BROWN, GERALD, editors. "The American Past." New York: The Macmillan Company, 1961.

FLEMING, THOMAS. "1776 Year of Illusions." Edison, New Jersey: Castle Books, 1996.

FLEXNER, JAMES THOMAS. "George Washington and the New Nation." Boston: Little, Brown and Co., 1969.

FLEXNER, JAMES THOMAS. "George Washington and the American Revolution." Boston: Little, Brown and Company, 1967.

FLEXNER, JAMES THOMAS. "Washington The Indispensable Man." Boston: Little, Brown and Company, 1969.

FOLSOM, BURTON W. JR., editor. "The Spirit of Freedom Essays in American History" New York: The Foundation for Economic Education, 1994.

FONER, ERIC. "Story of the American Freedom." New York: W.W. Norton and Company, 1998.

FREEMAN, DOUGLAS SOUTHALL. "George Washington." New York: Charles Scribner's and Sons, 1951.

FREEMAN, DOUGLAS SOUTHALL. "Washington." New York: Simon and Schuster, 1948.

GARRATY, JOHN. "The American Nation." New York: American Heritage Publishing Co. Inc., 1966.

GREGG, GARY and SPALDING, MATTHEW, editors "Patriot Sage." Wilmington Delaware: ISI Books, 1999.

GRIZZARD, FRANK, JR. "George Washington, A Biographical Companion." Santa Barbara, Calif: ABC-CLIO, Inc., 2002.

HENRIQUES, PETER. "The Death of George Washington." Mt. Vernon: Mt. Vernon Ladies Association, 2000.

HIGGINBOTHAM, DON. "The War of American Independence." Boston: Northeastern University Press, 1983.

HIRSCHFIELD, FRITZ. "George Washington and Slavery." Columbia, Missouri: University of Missouri Press, 1997.

HUMPHREYS, DAVID. "Life of General Washington." Athens, Ga.: University of Georgia Press, 1991.

IRVING, WASHINGTON. "Life of George Washington." New York: The Co-operative Publication Society, Inc. 1859.

ISELY, BLISS. "The Horseman of the Shenandoah." Milwaukee: Bruce Publishing Company, 1962.

JAFFE, IRMA. "John Trumbull." New York: New York Graphic Society, 1975.

JOHNSON, PAUL. "A History of the American People." New York: Harper Collins Publishers, 1997.

JONES, ROBERT. "George Washington." New York: Fordham University Press, 2002.

KETCHUM, RICHARD. "Saratoga." New York: Henry Holt and Co, Inc., 1997.

KOCH, ADRIENNE. "The American Enlightenment." New York: George Braziller, 1965.

LIND, MICHAEL, editor. "Hamilton's Republic." New York: The Free Press, 1997.

LONGMORE, PAUL K. "The Invention of George Washington." Berkeley: University or California Press. 1988.

LUCAS, STEPHEN. "The Quotable George Washington." Madison, Wisconsin: Madison House Publishers, Inc., 1999.

MAIER, PAULINE. "American Scripture." London: Pimlico, 1999.

MARTIN, JAMES and STUBAUS, KAREN. "The American Revolution: Whose Revolution?" Huntington, New York: Robert E. Krieger Publishing Company, 1981.

MARTIN, JOSEPH PLUMB. "Ordinary Courage." St. James, N.Y. Brandywine Press, 1993.

MCCULLIOUGH, DAVID. "John Adams." New York: Simon and Schuster, 2001.

MCFARLAND, PHILIP. "The Brave Bostonians." Boulder, Colorado: Westview Press, 1998.

MEIRS, EARL, Editor. "The American Story." Great Neck, New York, 1956.

MILLARD, CATHERINE. "Great American Statesmen and Heroes." Camp Hill, Pa.: Horizon Books, 1995.

MILLARD, CATHERINE. "The Rewriting of American History." Camp Hill, Pa.: Horizon Books, 1991.

MILLER, JOHN C. "Origins of the American Revolution." Boston: Little, Brown and Company, 1943.

MORGAN, EDMUND. "Prologue to Revolution." Raleigh, North Carolina, 1959.

MORGAN, EDMUND. "The Birth of the Republic 1763-89." Chicago: The University of Chicago Press, 1956.

MORGAN, EDMUND. “The Genius of George Washington.” New York: W.W. Norton Company, 1977.

MORISON, SAMUEL ELIOT. “John Paul Jones.” Alexandria, Va.: Time Life Books, 1959.

MORISON, SAMUEL ELIOT. “The Oxford History of the American People.” New York: Oxford University Press, 1965.

O’BRIEN, CONOR CRUISE. “The Long Affair.” London: Pimlico, 1998.

RAKOVE, JACK. “Original Meanings.” New York: Alfred A. Knopf, 1997.

RANDALL, WILLARD STERNE. “George Washington.” New York: Henry Holt and Company, 1997.

RHODEHAMEL, JOHN. “The Great Experiment.” New Haven: Yale University Press, 1998.

ROGERS, L. RANDALL. “Our Masonic Presidents.” Waco: Texian Press, 1998.

ROSENFIELD, RICHARD. “American Aurora.” New York: St. Martin’s Griffin, 1997.

SCHEER, GEORGE and RANKIN, HUGH. “Rebels and Redcoats.” New York: Da Capo Press, Inc., 1957.

SCHLESINGER, ARTHUR and FOX, DIXON. “A History of American Life.” New York: Scribner, 1996.

SCHOULER, JAMES. “Americans of 1776, Gansevoort, N.Y.: Corner House Historical Publications, 1995.

SHEEHAN, DONALD. “The Making of American History.” New York: The Dryden Press, 1958.

SMITH, PAGE. “John Adams.” New York: Doubleday and Company, Inc., 1962.

SMITH, RICHARD NORTON. “Patriach.” Boston: Houghton Mifflin Company, 1991.

STILES, T. J., editor. “ In Their Own Words.” New York: A Perigee Book, 1999.

TERBEL, JOHN. “Turning the World Upside Down.” New York: Orion Books, 1993.

THACHER, JAMES M.D. “Military Journal of the American Revolution 1775-1783.” Gansevoort, New York: Corner House Historical Publications, 1998.

THOMAS, HENRY and THOMAS, DANA. “50 Great Americans.” Garden City, NY: Doubleday and Company, Inc., 1948.

TUCHMAN, BARBARA. “The First Salute.” New York; Ballantine Books, 1988.

TWOHIG, DOROTHY, editor. “George Washington Diaries.” Charlottesville: University of Virginia Press, 1999.

WASHINGTON, GEORGE. “The Journal of George Washington.” Williamsburg: Colonial Williamsburg, 1959.

WEST, THOMAS. “Vindicating the Founders.” New York: Rowman and Littlefield Publishers, Inc. 1997.

WILLS, GARRY. “George Washington and the Enlightenment.” London: Robert Hale, 1984.

WILLS, GARRY. “James Madison.” New York: Henry Holt and Company, 2002.

WOOD, GORDON. “The Radicalism of the American Revolution.” New York: Alfred Knopf, 1991.

Leadership Books

ADAMS, BOB. “The Everything Leadership Book.” Holbrook, Mass.: Adams Media Corporation, 2001.

ASHKENAS, RON; ULRICH ,DAVE; JICK, TODD and KERR, STEVE. “The Boundaryless Organization.” San Francisco: Jossey-Bass, 2002.

AXELROD, ALAN. “Patton on Leadership.” Paramus: Prentice Hall Press, 1999.

BENDER, PETER URS and TOROK, GEORGE. “Secrets of Power Marketing.” New York: Stoddard Publishing Co., 2000.

BENNIS, WARREN and BIEDERMAN, PATRICI WARD. "Organizing Genius." Reading, Mass. Addison-Wesley Publishing Co., 1997.

BENNIS, WARREN and GODSMITH, JOAN, "Learning to Lead." Cambridge: Perseus Books, 1997.

BENNIS, WARREN and MANUS, BURT. "Leaders." New York: Harper and Row, 1985.

BENNIS, WARREN and NANUS, BURT. "Leaders, The Strategies For Taking Charge." New York: and Row Publishers, 1985.

BENNIS, WARREN and TOWNSEND, ROBERT. "Reinventing Leadership." New York: William Morrow and Co., 1995.

BENNIS, WARREN. "On Becoming a Leader." Reading, Mass. Addison-Wesley Publishing Co. Inc., 1989.

BENNIS, WARREN. "On Becoming a Leader." Reading: Perseus Books, 1989.

BENNIS, WARREN; SPRITZER,GRETHEN and CUMMING,THOMAS. "The Future of Leadership." San Franscisco: Jossey-Bass, 2001.

BIRO, BRIAN. "Beyond Success." New York: A Perigee Book, 1977.

BLANCHARD, KEN. "DNA Leadership Through Goal-Driven Management." Reston, VA: The goals institute, 1997.

BLANCHARD, KEN. "Heart of a Leader." Escondido: Ken Blanchard Companies, 1990.

BOWLES, SHELDON and BLANCHARD, KENNETH. "Raving Fans." New York: William Morrow and Company, Inc., 1993.

BURNS, JAMES MACGREGOR. "Transforming Leadership." New York: Atlantic Monthly Press, 2003.

BUSHE, GERVASE. "Clear Leadership." Palo Alto: Davies-Black Publications, 2001.

CAMPBELL, ANDREW and NASH, LAURA. “A Sense of Mission.” New York: Addison-Wesley Publishing Co., 1990.

CANNON, JEFF. “Leadership Lessons Of The Navy Seals.” New York: McGraw Hill, 2002.

COHEN, WILLIAM. “The New Art Of The Leader.” Paramus: Prentice Hall Press, 2000.

COLES, ROBERT, editor. “The Erik Erikson Reader.” New York: W.W. Norton and Company, 2000.

COVEY, STEPHEN. “First Things First.” New York: Simon and Schuster, 1994.

COVEY, STEPHEN. “Principle-Centered Leadership.” New York: A Fireside Book, 1990.

COWAN, JOHN. “Techniques for Communicators.” Chicago: Lawrence Ragan Communications, Inc., 1992.

CROCKER, H.W. “Robert E. Lee on Leadership.” Rocklin, Ca.: Prima Publishing, 1999.

CROSBY, PHILLIP B. “Leading.” New York: McGraw- Hill Inc., 1990.

DANIELS, AUBREY C. “Bringing out the Best in People.” New York: McGraw-Hill, Inc., 1994.

DANZIG, ROBERT J. “The Leader Within You.” Hollywood, Florida: Lifetime Books Inc., 1998.

DAWSON, ROGER. “The Thirteen Secrets of Power Performance.” Englewood Cliffs, N.J: Prentice Hall, Inc., 1994.

DUBRIN, ANDREW. “Idiots Guide to Leadership” Indianapolis: Alpha Books, 2000.

ELLET, WILLIAM. “A Critical Guide to Management Training Media.” Boston: Harvard Business School, 1997.

FARHAR,CHARLES and DE BACKER, PHILIPPE. “Maximum Leadership.” New York: Henry Holt and Co., 1996.

GATTO, REX P. PH.D. “Teamwork through Flexible Leadership.” Pittsburgh: GTA Press, 1992.

GEORGE, CARL F. "Nine Keys to Effective Small Group Leadership." Mansfield, Pa. Kingdom Publishing, 1997.

GERBER, ROBIN. "Leading the Eleanor Roosevelt Way." New York: Prentice Hall, 2002.

GREENLEAF, ROBERT K. "Servant Leadership." New York: Paulist Press, 1977.

HARARI, OREN. "Leadership Secrets of Colin Powell." New York: McGraw-Hill, 2002.

HAWLEY, JACK. "Reawakening the Spirit in Work." San Francosco: Berrett-Koehler Publishers, 1993.

HEIDER, JOHN. "The Tao of Leadership." Atlanta: Humanics New Age, 1985.

HEIFETZ,RONALD and LINSKY, MARTY. "Leadership On The Line." Boston: Harvard Business School Press, 2002.

HEIL ,GARY; PARKER, TOM and TATE, RICK. "Leadership and the Customer Revolution." New York: Van Nostrand Reinhold, 1995.

HERMAN, STANLEY. "The Tao at Work." San Francisco: Jossey–Bass, 1994.

HESSELBEIN, Frances. "Hesselbein on Leadership" San Francisco: Jossey-Bass, 2002.

JAWORSKI, JOSEPH. "Synchronicity." San Francisco: Berrett-Koehler, 1996.

JAY, ANTONY. "Management and Machiavelli." Amsterdam: Pfeiffer and Company, 1994.

KOTTER, JOHN P. "A Force for Change." New York: The Free Press, 1990.

KOTTER, JOHN P. "Leading Change. Boston: Harvard Business School Press, 1996.

KOUZER, JAMES and POSNER, BARRY. "The Leadership Challenge." San Francisco: Jorsey-Bass, 2002.

KOUZES, JAMES. "Business Leadership." San Francisco, Jossey-Bass, 2003.

KUCZMARSKI, SUSAN and THOMAS. "Values Based Leadership." Englewood, N.J: Prentice Hall, 1995.

LEVINE, STUART and CROM, MICHAEL. "The Leader in You." New York: Simon and Schuster, 1993.

LOEB, MARSHALL and KINDEL, STEPHEN. "Leadership for Dummies." Foster City, CA.: IDG Books, 1999.

LOMBARDI, VINCE JR. "What it Takes to Be #1." New York: R.R. Donnelly, 2001.

MAXWELL, JOHN. "Laws of Leadership." Nashville: Thomas Nelson, Inc., 1998.

MCCORMACK, MARK. "What They Still Don't Teach You At Harvard Business School." New York: Bantam Books, 1989.

MUIRHEAD, BRIAN SIMON WILLIAM. "High Velocity Leadership." New York: Harper Business, 1999.

NANUS, BURT. "Visionary Leadership." San Francisco: Jossey-Bass, 1992.

NELSON, BOB and ECONOMY, PETER. "Managing for Dummies." Foster City, CA. IDG Books, 1996.

O'TOOLE, JAMES. "Leadership A to Z." San Francisco: Jossey-Bass Publishers, 1999.

PETERS, TOM. "Seminar." New York: Vantage Books, 1994.

PHILLIPS, DONALD. "Lincoln on Leadership." New York: Warner Books, 1992.

ROBBINS, ANTHONY. "Awaken the Giant Within." New York: Summit Books, 1991.

ROBBINS, ANTHONY. "Unlimited Power." New York; Fireside, 1997.

ROBERTS, WESS. "The Best Advice Ever for Leaders." Kansas City: Andrews Mc Neel Publishing, 2002.

STEVENS, MARK. "Extreme Management." New York: Time Warner Books, 2001.

STORR, ANTHONY, "The Essential Jung" Princeton: Princeton University Press, 1983.

TERRY, ROBERT W. "Authentic Leadership." San Francisco: Jossey-Bass Publishers, 1993.

TICHY, NOEL and DEVANNA, MARY ANNE. "The Transformational Leader." New York: John Wiley and Sons, 1986.

TICHY, NOEL. "The Leadership Engine." New York: Harper Collins Publishers, 1997.

ULRICH, DAVE; ZENGER JACK and SMALLWOOD, NORM. "Results Based Leaderhship." Boston: Harvard Business School Press, 1999.

ULRICK, ZENGER and SMALLWOOD. "Results Based Leadership." Boston: Harvard Business School Press, 1999.

WALTON, MARY. "The Deming Management Method." New York: a Perigee Book, 1986.

WHITE, HODGSON, and CRAINER. "The Future of Leadership." London: Pitman Publishing . 1996.

WICK, CALHOUN and LEON, LU STANTON. "The Learning Edge." New York: McGraw-Hill , Inc., 1993.

ZENGER, JOHN AND FOLKMAN, JOSEPH. "The Extraordinary Leader." New York: McGraw Hill, 2002.

Index

How To Order This Book

By email: james@leadershipbygeorge.com

By U.S Mail: **James Parrish Hodges**
824 Olympic Ave.
Edmonds, WA 98020
425-673-2525

By Phone:

I understand I may return this book for a full refund, for any reason no questions asked.

Please send me free information on your other books, articles, speaking, consulting and coaching

Name ______________________________

Address ______________________________

City/State/Zip ______________________________

Telephone ______________________________

E-mail address ______________________________

Payment: Check or Credit Card

Card number ______________________________

Name on card/exp date

____